THE COMPLETE GUIDE TO NEWFOUNDLAND DOGS

Katie Dolan

Publication Data

Katie Dolan

The Complete Guide to Newfoundland Dogs – First edition.

Summary: "Successfully raising a Newfoundland Dog from puppy to old age"

– Provided by publisher.

ISBN: 978-1-954288-56-0

[1. Newfoundland Dog – Non-Fiction] I. Title.

Design by Sorin Rădulescu
First paperback edition, 2022
Author photo on the back cover provided by: Alonso Nichols/Tufts University

TABLE OF CONTENTS

CHAPTER 6

Training Your Newfoundland **59**

CHAPTER 7

Exercise **73**

CHAPTER 8

Socializing Your Newfoundland **81**

CHAPTER 9

Nutrition 91

CHAPTER 10

Health 97

Photo Courtesy
of Heidi Peterson

Special Thanks

With thanks to the many Newfoundland Club of America members, breeders, friends, and colleagues at the Tufts Cummings School of Veterinary Medicine who made suggestions and offered advice as this book was whelped. A special thanks to Karen Steinrock, my collaborator, friend, and content expert who generously shared her ideas and network of NCA contacts. Additional thanks to my friend and talented Bernese Mountain Dog breeder Linda Seaver, who carefully read an early draft, and to Kathy Kosierowski, a great dog trainer.

Many Newfoundland Club of America and regional club members contributed images, quotes, and ideas for the book. Thanks to Clyde Dunphy, Marylou Zimmerman, Betty McDonnell, Becky Reynnells, Peggy Helming, Sheila Mallinson, Benita Edds, Patti Sutherland, Cathy Derench, Amy Culver Davis, Katie Stankey, Megan Goldin, Jessica Hoffman, Mary Bylone, Dwight Gorsuch, Judith Ziffer, Cissy Sullivan, Marie Acosta, Sabrina Conci, Heidi Peterson, Gary Baldwin, Suzanne Jones, Sue Auger, Jeana Yager, Cece Guyatt, Penny Shubert, Judi Adler, Jenni Lott, and Laurel Rabschutz.

I can't thank the Newfoundland Club of America enough for their help with this book. The advice and input from their many members helped make this project a success. Their website is an excellent resource for any first-time (or veteran) Newfoundland owner. The pages contain a wealth of knowledge and expert advice, as well as the gateway into a wonderful community of Newf owners who truly love this incredible breed.

Katie

Visit the Newfoundland
Club of America at
www.ncanewfs.org

PREFACE

As you'll discover from reading this book, the science surrounding canine nutrition, training, exercise, and veterinary interventions continues to evolve. Research and long-term studies have only recently been funded to answer key questions about the optimal age to spay/neuter, dog food and its ingredients, and other unresolved controversies among people of goodwill in the canine world.

Drawing on the expertise of breeders, veterinarians, researchers, groomers, behaviorists, and trainers, this book describes the current available science and reliable resources for finding information. Undoubtedly, future findings will make some of this information obsolete. As you embark as a Newfoundland owner, please stay informed and updated for your peace of mind and for your dog's health and happiness. I've tried to include trustworthy websites, but social media is rife with misinformation. Trust reputable breeders, veterinarians, and dog food manufacturers.

Because some Canadians consider "Newfie" a slur for the people of Newfoundland, I've chosen to use the words Newf or Newfy when informally referring to the breed. In addition, because so many of us have deep connections with our dogs, I've used the pronouns she or he when referring to a single Newfoundland.

Throughout the book, where appropriate (or humorous), I've included stories about our dear Newfoundlands. The cast of characters: Bella, who had a litter of puppies when she was three and lived until she was nearly 12 years of age; Blue, her son; and Willow, our new puppy who joined the family in late 2021. You can read more about Bella in the Epilogue and in her Wildlife Ambassador books.

Completing the final book edits, I realize these pages contain many "Thou Shall Nots," strong suggestions, and warnings. As a counterbalance, I've included joyous stories about goofy Newfs. I readily acknowledge we've made mistakes along the way, and I hope you can avoid some of the errors we've made. However, we've enjoyed every minute of our Newf-related

Photo Courtesy of Amy Lange

activities, beginning with a cold nose wake up at 5:30 a.m., mealtimes, play times, selecting a hiking adventure, grooming, snacks, obedience, picking up poop, and walking them at night right before bedtime. We know you will love and enjoy your sweet Newf too.

Katie Dolan

CHAPTER 1

A Sweet, Versatile Working Dog and Companion

A Bit about Newfoundlands

"I used to have dogs, now I have Newfoundlands," writes breeder and author Rhoda Lehrman. Rhoda adds, *"Today's Newfs are gentle, adoring, powerful, with excellent judgment. They have sweet expressions and loving eyes, a long, flowing coat, and a huge round head...Where does such a creature come from? What a gift to live with a powerful animal whose work is to save our lives."*

What a gift indeed! We've had large purebred and mixed-breed dogs since I was a child, but nurturing Bella, my first Newfoundland, raising and finding good homes for Bella's litter of eight, and many years of owning Newfoundlands Bella, Blue, and Willow, made me fall in love with these gentle, people-focused giants.

Famous Newfoundland dogs, both fictional and real, include shaggy Nana from *Peter Pan*; Seaman, the dog who accompanied the Lewis and Clark expedition; the elegant black and white dogs featured in Edward Landseer's oil paintings; and Gander, the World War II hero who protected Canadian soldiers before being killed in battle while gathering a grenade and was posthumously awarded the prestigious Dickin Medal. These famous and noble creatures are only part of the story. Newfoundlands, harkening from the cold north Atlantic coast, originally worked to bring in fishing nets, and over the centuries, hauled wood and other materials, rescued drowning people, turned heavy wheels, and have done a variety of other jobs. In today's world, Newfoundlands continue to love work. They are big, messy, often drool, require regular grooming, and thrive in a home where they can be with their people.

Photo Courtesy of Jessica Hoffman

Village Dogs and Breeds

Let's consider Newfoundlands and other dog breeds in the context of canines around the world. Village dogs, who number over a billion worldwide, are not "owned" in the traditional sense of a pet living in a home. Ray Coppinger and other canine researchers distinguish between confined dogs that have their fertility restricted (pets) and village dogs free to wander and select mates. Over time, selective local breeding created specific landraces (dogs with distinct, defined traits) in each watershed across Europe and Africa. The currently registered dog breeds are all less than two centuries old, representing selective mating to replicate certain desirable traits. Only fourteen breeds formally existed in 1788, while over 400 breeds are currently recognized around the world.

The history of the Newfoundland dog is uncertain. Apparently, French fishermen visited Newfoundland in the 1500s and brought Great Pyrenees dogs, which were likely mixed with the sporting dogs brought by the English. During the 1880s, travelers to Newfoundland reported the island had two types of dogs: the smaller St. John's Dog or the Lesser Newfoundland, ancestor of today's Labrador Retriever, and the heavier, longer-coated Greater Newfoundland, ancestor of my dogs. Today, approximately 3,000 purebred Newfoundlands are born annually in the United States, and the breed ranks 40th in popularity, according to the American Kennel Club.

A Proud History in Water Rescue

Each dog breed, after generations of selection for a variety of genetic traits, has a unique "instinctual intelligence." For the Newfoundland, it is a superb water rescue instinct, although not every Newfoundland likes swimming. The original dogs helped cod fishermen pull in heavy nets in the cold North Atlantic seas by swimming out to a net buoy, grabbing it, and bringing it back to the boat. Newfoundland dogs were often stationed at lighthouses, considered to be part of the regular rescue equipment. Stories about Newfoundland rescues abound. A dog named Hairyman helped rescue 160 Irish immigrants from a shipwreck in the early 1800s. Swansea Jack saved dozens of shipwreck victims, and a Newfoundland allegedly rescued Napoleon Bonaparte when a large wave knocked the general into the water near the island of Elba.

A double-layered coat traps air and makes the dog more buoyant, while a thick tail acts as a rudder. Webbed feet help power a Newf through the water. Big jowls help keep water out of the dog's mouth when a swimming Newfoundland rescues people or brings back a buoy. A well-trained Newf can simultaneously assess several drowning victims and, like a calm emergency room triage nurse, decide which victim needs rescue first. The dog will swim past another victim, heading

Photo Courtesy of Heidi Peterson

for the person most in need of a shaggy shoulder. Using its powerful feet, the Newfoundland can pull the drowning victim toward shore.

Over the years, I've often swum in the warm summer ocean on the coast of Rhode Island. When I'd finish a swim, rounding the last jagged point and heading toward shore, my Newfoundland Bella would leap off the rock where she'd waited and rush to "rescue" me. I'd grab the fur on her back near her shoulders and let her pull me ashore. One time, as I dried Bella and myself off, I saw two tall ships on the horizon, heading to a celebratory gathering in Boston. The ships were majestic, with tall, dark masts and massive white sails running before the wind. I considered that three centuries ago, Bella's ancestor might have been stationed on one of those vessels. As a Newfoundland, she nobly represented a proud seafaring history.

Photo Courtesy of Dylan Hattem

Dog expert Stanley Coren analyzed over 1,000 news reports about dog heroism. According to his analysis, Newfs and St. Bernards account for 20% of all water rescues reported. His dog behavior inventory lists Newfoundlands in the draft dog group with the following rankings: very low on dominance, moderately high on intelligence, very low on emotional reactivity, very high on sociability, and very low on energy level.

Attempts to expand the breed's rescue résumé have sometimes been misguided. In the early 1900s, the Paris Police added several Newfoundland dogs to their force, hoping the dogs would thwart robbers swimming the Seine and rescue attempted suicide victims. The *chiens plongeurs* (diving dogs), purchased as adult dogs, were inexpertly trained. It showed: the dogs had little impulse control. One dog rescued a ham hock floating down the river and devoured it. A thief thwarted his canine pursuers by throwing sausage and bread on the ground. A suicide attempt was, indeed, prevented, but the victim had large bruises from being manhandled by his Newfoundland rescuer. After several negative newspaper articles and a cartoon suggesting the dog squad was a version of the Keystone Cops (the bumbling French policemen in silent films of the 1910s), the experiment was abandoned.

Photo Courtesy of The Zimmerman Collection

SAVED

Crossbreeding to create rescue dogs has led to other problems. The Moscow Water Dog was, for a brief period, the Russian version of a Newfoundland. The Russian Navy wanted to create a water rescue dog after many service dogs were lost in World War II, so several Newfoundlands were brought from Germany and crossed with small, terrier-like Russian breeds. The dogs were large and swam well. When tested with naval personnel, however, a Moscow Water Dog swam out through crashing waves with its powerful webbed feet toward the thrashing, pretend "victim." The dog approached and bit the stunned, swimming sailor, who then truly became a victim. The Moscow Water Dog is now extinct.

During World War I, some of the best Newfoundlands in England were poisoned by a crank who supposedly thought the dogs were taking food needed by soldiers. In fact, large dogs were often sacrificed during the wars due to the enforcement of strict rules about pet ownership to protect food supplies in trying times. With the demise of the Gypsy line of English dogs and the inbreeding of the few remaining Newfoundlands in Great Britain, the focus on preserving the breed shifted to North America, and the Newfoundland Club of America was established.

Hearth Dogs

Newfoundlands are sometimes referred to as "hearth dogs" as they love being indoors with their human companions. Several United States presidents have owned Newfoundlands as companions. Bobby Kennedy's Newfoundland Brumus was "oversized and under-supervised" when he went to work with his owner. A 2022 survey of Newfoundland breeders emphasized that the human connection is critical to a Newf's happiness. My Newfs follow me around the house and, as fellow breeder Dr. Judith Ziffer writes, *"They love nothing better than to be included with their humans in daily activities. The more time Newfs get to spend with members of their family, the more they thrive. If their human is ready for a nap, they are always ready to join in. If the activity is Frisbee or chasing a ball, Newfs are enthusiastic to join the play."* Throughout this book, you'll often read about the time, grooming, training, effort, and love that a Newfoundland requires from its owner.

Photo Courtesy of Katie Dolan

Versatile Working Dogs

Although they love to lounge by the hearth, Newfs also thrive through working. Today, Newfoundlands compete in draft, obedience, water rescue, conformation (show dog), and, despite their size and clumsiness, agility. Newfs make excellent therapy dogs and have even learned to truffle hunt, as Marylou Zimmerman of Seattle reports. One of her Newfs came back from the forest with truffle breath from eating mushrooms. After sharing a bit of the delicacy, her other dogs started looking for truffles in the forest.

Photo Courtesy of Marie Acosta

Newfoundlands in Literature and Art

As gentle giants with a noble bearing, Newfoundlands have been popular in the arts. The breed is immortalized in sculptures depicting heroic acts and frequently appears in Charles Dickens's novels, although Dickens was apparently not always kind to his giant dogs. Carlo, a dog narrator popular in British literature of the 1800s, is "descended both by the father's and mother's side from the noble race of Newfoundland dogs." Scottish Poet Robert Burns refers to the breed as "the gentleman scholar." Mark Twain expands on this theme in his unfinished 1920 "Letters from a Dog to Another Dog Explaining and Accounting for Man," written by "author" Newfoundland Smith. The dog narrator is an educated gentleman writing to a colleague; his writing is interrupted when he rescues a boy who falls into the river. The half-drunk father tears the Newfoundland's ear as punishment after his son falsely claims the big dog pushed him into the river. The reader ponders the fundamental unfairness and incongruity between the expected praise and a thrashing, while also admiring the nobility of the Newfoundland.

*Photo Courtesy
of The Zimmerman Collection*

One of Emily Dickinson's poems begins, "I started Early – Took my Dog – And visited the Sea." Dickinson writes of her "shaggy ally" Carlo, a Newfoundland, *"I talk of all these things with Carlo, and his eyes grow meaning, and his shaggy feet keep a slower pace."* Carlo made an "intermittent Plush" sound while walking beside her. (My Bella made that sound when dragging her paws through the sand.) Meanwhile, Milo, a black and white Newfoundland from Nahant, Massachusetts, rescued several children and was immortalized by Edward Landseer. Landseer painted black and white Newfoundlands, popularizing and lending his name to the recessive coat color.

Let's circle back to the lyrical Rhoda Lehrman. After the birth of a gigantic litter of seventeen puppies to her Newfoundland dam, she writes, *"The puppies in our home that first night carried ancient noble blood, had the potential of greatness, kindness, and wisdom: souls. I could not feel more responsibility. I had brought them into the world through my decision, and it was up to me to defend them from error, illness, cold, hunger, accident, stupidity, laziness. They were my burden, and a terrible burden it was. I couldn't wait until they looked into my eyes and showed me the blossom of their souls."* That sums up what it is like to own a Newfoundland dog.

CHAPTER 2
Physical and Personality Traits

Sweet, sturdy, solid, and sensitive are top-of-mind words when it comes to the physical traits and personality of the Newfoundland. The previous chapter showcased the Newfoundland's work ethic and versatility, but how has the breed been developed to serve its owners in such diverse ways? The breed standard provides clues as to how and why generations of Newfs have been bred to be versatile working dogs.

Photo Courtesy of Heidi Peterson

Photo Courtesy of Katie Dolan

The Breed Standard

The Newfoundland Club of America's breed standard begins with the most important attribute, stating, "The Newfoundland is a sweet-dispositioned dog that acts neither dull nor ill-tempered" and ends with the words, "Sweetness of temperament is the hallmark of the Newfoundland: this is the most important single characteristic of the breed." Indeed, the Newfoundland standard is the only breed standard that begins with the dog's distinguishing gentle giant personality.

The standard then highlights key physical attributes: large, heavily coated, deep-bodied, slightly longer than tall, a massive head and broad skull, small and triangular ears, dark brown eyes, and a clean-cut muzzle. "The expression is soft and reflects the characteristics of the breed: benevolence, intelligence, and dignity." The average height for an adult male is 28 inches with an average weight of 130–150 pounds, while females are slightly smaller at an average height of 26 inches with an average weight of 100 to 120 pounds.

A Newf's neck, topline, tail, forequarters, and hindquarters, as well as the gait, are also described. Newfoundlands have a double coat, with a coarse outer layer over a soft and dense undercoat. Recognized colors are black, brown, gray, and white/black. The Landseer has a white base coat with black markings. Landseers (European Continental Type) are a distinct breed in Europe (bred to look like the dog painted by Edwin Landseer) and are judged separately by the European Kennel Clubs. American Landseers, with recessive coat color genes, are often crossbred with black Newfs to promote genetic diversity and health.

Learning about the Standard

On my first foray to the annual Newfoundland National Specialty, I joined 80 breeders in a large conference room, sitting in folding chairs around a Westminster-like green floor covering. We were staying in a rambling Pennsylvania hotel specializing in hosting dog-related events. It had wide lawns, plenty of parking for trailers, and musty corridors. A handwritten sign indicated dogs were not allowed in the bar but otherwise had free rein. Nearly everyone had a Newfoundland by her side. I missed my Bella, who would have loved the other dogs and all the doggy smells.

Pat Hastings, the seminar presenter, was well known within the rarified world of breeders. She spoke with a slight Southern accent. She reviewed the Newfoundland breed standard line by line, discussing size, structure, substance, and other important traits. A gentle temperament is paramount. Incorrect temperament is genetic. Breeders say, "bites will come back to bite you." A Newfoundland carries 60% of its weight on its furry forearms. These legs are "columns of support," which should be neither fiddle-fronted (front elbows and feet splayed out) nor cow-hocked (hind legs splayed out). A Newfoundland should be slightly longer than it is tall, differing from a poodle's perfect square and length matching height. Although all dogs have 13 pairs of ribs, the curvature and shape vary. A Newfoundland's rib cage is oval. "You don't want too much daylight under a dog, but you do want the dog to cover the ground well."

The speaker discussed the difference between a topline (ears to tail) and a backline (end of withers to tail). We studied the stop, the point where a dog's muzzle meets its forehead. A Golden Retriever needs an adequate stop to see while carrying a bird in its mouth, while a Newfoundland needs a pronounced stop so it can swim with a buoy in its mouth. Overall, the breed standards can, to the novice, seem like the canine version of Da Vinci's calculations of a perfect human body's proportions. After 90 minutes of the dense, information-packed lecture, my head swam with new terminology and concepts. Indeed, I developed a headache behind my stop and decided it was time for bed!

The next day, I wandered around the show, watching handsome dogs patiently waiting on grooming tables as their double coats were teased, fluffed, and snipped. Drool bibs were among the many Newfoundland items for sale; I was glad that my Bella was generally not a big drooler. Many people bring their dogs to the Nationals but do not show them in the ring. All the people and all the Newfs were friendly. No one asked before petting a dog; it was assumed the dogs were calm and friendly, as the breed standard mandates.

Notable Newfoundland Breeders

The Newfoundland Club of America website notes that Elizabeth Loring's Waseeka Kennel was the first large Newfoundland kennel in the United States, but she was soon joined in her ground-breaking breeding efforts by Dryad Kennels and Coastwise Kennels. These three kennels are considered the foundation kennels for the American Newfoundland. Camayer Kennels helped to reestablish the Landseer and reversed the declining

Photo Courtesy of Ashbey Photographers

Josh winning Best in Show at Westminster in 2004

Photo Courtesy of Peggy Helming

Josh reading his fan mail after Westminster win

Landseer numbers. Mrs. Ayers-Jameson later changed the kennel name to Seaward. The Kennel would produce some of the 20th century's greatest Newfoundlands, including Ch. Seaward's Blackbeard or "Adam," the most winning Newf of his time and the first Newf to claim Best in Show at Westminster in 1984. In recent years, the Newfoundland again caught the public's eye when Ch. Darbydale's All Rise Pouch Cove or "Josh" became the second Newf to gain the Westminster Best in Show in 2004.

> **"**
>
> *Josh was one of 12 puppies in his litter. The balance and fluid harmony that he showed in the ring was there when he was still a puppy. Add to that his irresistible personality and we had a real champion.*
>
> PEGGY HELMING
> *Pouch Cove Newfoundlands*
>
> **"**

More about the Newf Personality

Let's explore the Newfoundland personality a bit more. The dog's sweet temperament and people-focus often translate into sensitivity. Newfs want to please and do not do well with negative reinforcement of any sort. A Newf prefers to be with its people and will not thrive if left alone for long periods of time. One breeder told me that many potential puppy owners (PPOs) called her during the early days of the recent pandemic, wanting to get a dog while they were working from home. She explained that she would not sell them a Newf because the dog would not adjust well when the potential owner returned to work.

Is a Newfoundland the Right Dog for You?

If you are considering adding a Newf to your family, your home should have people around. Reputable breeders will ask about your lifestyle, wanting to ensure the dog is not left alone all day. Think about who will train and nurture a puppy and grown dog. You also will need to accept that the

Photo Courtesy of Katie Dolan

18

Photo Courtesy
of Jeana Yager

average life expectancy is eight to ten years, although healthy Newfs can live many more years than the average. Smaller dogs, with genes that promote longevity, will live longer on average. Some potential owners feel the adage about Newfoundland life expectancy—three years a young dog, three years a good dog, three years an old dog— is simply too short, with too many goodbyes. In addition, Newfoundlands are susceptible to numerous health issues (See Chapter 13), so veterinary bills can be expensive. The biggest health concerns for the breed are cardiac issues, orthopedic problems (due to their size), cancers, bloat, and eye issues.

The other considerations almost go without saying. All Newfoundlands drool, although the amount of drool depends a bit on the lineage. Their double coat means lots of shedding and lots of grooming required. (See the grooming chapter.) The dogs love playing with water, and your Newf will inevitably find the puddles on a walk, then bring mud and dirt into your home. They are big and somewhat clumsy, much like the proverbial bull in a china shop. Their tails will sweep knickknacks off end tables. In sum, they are not good dogs for fastidious homemakers. And finally, Newfs mature slowly, with bones growing until two years of age. They are not a good choice for people who want to take their dogs on long runs. Even as adults, Newfs can overheat if they exercise for too long.

Photo Courtesy of Katie Dolan

On the other hand, the Newfy is great for families. They are typically good with children, other pets, and other animals. Newfs are also a good choice for people who desire a strong, intense relationship with their dog and for owners who want to do therapy, water rescue, and other working dog activities. Owning a Newf can also work well for people with more sedentary lifestyles who desire canine companionship, a nice walk, and perhaps an afternoon nap with a furry beast.

CHAPTER 3
Finding Your Newfoundland

Research, referrals, red flags, and rescues are words describing the often-lengthy process of finding the right Newfoundland for your family. A successful search is going to take time, patience, and energy. Some of the most sought-after breeders have long waiting lists, so be patient and persistent. Spend time learning about Newfs and reputable breeders. Learn about the red flags for puppy mills and disreputable breeders. Accurately describe your lifestyle and family. Trust the breeder to know the puppies.

Photo Courtesy of Katie Dolan

Explain what qualities you are looking for in your new family member, and let the breeder select the right puppy for your lifestyle. Pick a breeder who whelps the puppies in the house, where they can be exposed to all the noises and distractions of real life. You may also want to consider a rescue or an older dog.

Searching for a Newfoundland to add to your family is time-consuming, requiring perseverance and planning. When I lost my Bella

Photo Courtesy of Marie Acosta

last summer, I knew it would take dedicated effort to find a puppy, especially since I wanted a co-ownership agreement so I could breed the female if she passed her health clearances. I prepared a summary about my love of Newfoundlands and experience with the breed; a breeder friend told me I needed to get to the point immediately and include how I could help the breeder.

I sent emails, called breeders, called Bella's breeder, who has retired, had conversations with the breeders who responded, and sent breeders thank-you notes and copies of my Bella books. I kept a detailed spreadsheet on my contacts, with reminders to call back when an anticipated litter might be "on the ground." I viewed this effort as a part-time job, one of the five or six things I wanted to accomplish last year. Eventually, I connected with a very reputable breeder and obtained Willow, my lovely and sweet puppy.

How to Find a Reputable Breeder and Litters

Begin by learning all you can about the breed. Try to attend the Newfoundland National and events organized by the local clubs. You can find information about upcoming events on the Newfoundland Club of America (NCA) website and the Facebook pages of the local clubs. Contact a Newfoundland Ambassador (listed on the NCA website) to request a list of approved breeders/litters and any available adult Newfs. The NCA also

Photo Courtesy of Patti Sutherland

designates Breeders of Distinction, who have carefully bred dogs of high quality. The NCA provides links to available rescues through its regional clubs. Choose a breeder from the NCA's breeder list or from a list maintained by the local club to be assured a breeder meets established criteria and actively works to improve the breed.

The Breeder's Critical Roles

Breeders know the Newfoundland lineages and carefully select appropriate pairings of sires and dams to improve the health of the breed. Research also shows early experiences, even before birth, affect puppies. Petting a pregnant female produces more docile puppies. Petting activates the parasympathetic system, facilitating relaxation, digestion, and emotional attachment. Although many aspects of temperament and behavior are genetic, Michael W. Fox, a veterinarian, ethologist, and author, and other researchers have traced puppy problem behaviors and health to mothers being stressed during pregnancy.

Exposure to parasites, poor nutrition, chemicals, disease, drugs, extreme temperatures, or emotional stress experienced by a pregnant bitch can cause problems in her puppies. In addition, puppies in utero respond to their mother being petted and subsequently have a greater tolerance to handling when born. And, as we will see in the socialization chapter, a puppy's early life with its mother and siblings has a very large impact on its adult behaviors and health.

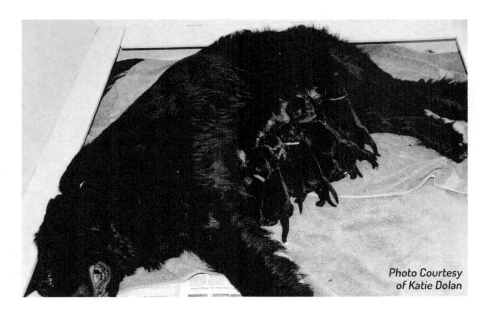

Photo Courtesy of Katie Dolan

Equally important are the early care of newborn puppies, the mother's teaching of her pups, and the socialization of pups with their littermates and the outside world. We'll learn more about these crucial elements in the chapter on socialization. A reputable breeder understands the importance of this early stage of a pup's life and the implications for its future health, happiness, and behaviors.

Red Flags

The Internet offers lists of bad breeder red flags, but I particularly like the one developed by Lisa Baldwin (developed for Bernese Mountain Dogs and reprinted below with permission) because it includes reasons why something might be a red flag in your search for a good breeder. Be leery of breeders who sell pups over the Internet or who don't require you to meet the puppy and the breeder, don't let you see where the puppies are being raised, don't allow you to meet the mother, raise puppies outside the home, don't adequately socialize the puppies, are licensed by the USDA (which has less stringent requirements than breed organizations), offer many breeds, don't ask questions about your family and commitment to the dogs, provide inadequate information about vaccinations and health screenings, don't agree to take a pup back, and have no association with the Newfoundland Club of America or regional breed clubs.

RED FLAGS

🚩🚩🚩	Why this is bad
Dogs are only listed by their call names.	Call names are simply the names that we use daily with our dogs. They are not unique. Every REGISTERED dog has a UNIQUE REGISTERED name. Using this registered name, you can check health clearances, health records, & titles on this dog through the Canine Health Information Center at the Orthopedics Foundation for Animals (www.ofa.org).
Breeder charges more for females, for registered vs. non-registered, or for full vs limited registration.	First you should not be charged more to have a registrable dog registered. This is simply unethical. If a breeder is selling a dog on limited registration, that means that the breeder feels that this dog should not be bred or shown in conformation. This judgment should not be overturned by an additional payment. And females cost the same to produce & raise as males.
Background information, such as pedigrees and health clearances are not available until AFTER you have paid a deposit.	Ethical breeders want you to have this information so that you can make an informed decision on whether this is the right litter for you. If a breeder is trying to conceal this information, that usually means that there is a problem. This would include breeders who get angry when you ask for documentation of health clearances.
Breeder's only questions revolve around payment & s/he discourages you from coming to their kennel. Breeder requires non-refundable deposit.	Responsible breeders want to meet the whole family & make sure that breed & individual puppy are a good fit. You want to see whether the dogs are kept in a safe & clean environment & how the puppies are being socialized.
Breeder sells puppies through third parties (brokers, dealers, retail shops, auctions)	Responsible breeders want to make sure that their puppies are going to the right homes. Then they are available to the puppy's buyers if they have problems (training, health) to give support and advice. Responsible breeders will take back any puppies they produce for the life of the dog.

(Reprinted with permission from Lisa Baldwin.)

Puppy Mills

This stark summary comes from an article by Lyle Davis. "Pet Store puppies most likely came from a large-scale, substandard commercial breeding operation, commonly known as a puppy mill. Puppy mills usually house dogs in overcrowded and unsanitary conditions, without adequate veterinary care, food, water, and socialization. The breeding stocks at puppy mills are bred as often as possible to increase profits. Starting at six months of age, the female is bred every heat cycle. She is often weak, malnourished, and dehydrated. The females are kept pregnant constantly but receive little veterinary care. The puppies produced are frequently of poor quality and ill health, taken too soon from their mothers and littermates to be shipped across the country to pet stores."

An increased incidence of behavioral disorders (fear and aggression toward other dogs and humans) has been documented in dogs bred by

Photo Courtesy of Marie Acosta

commercial breeders, puppy farms, and sold in pet stores (McMillan, 2017). Another study categorized breeders as "responsible" or "irresponsible" based on questions such as the number of available litters, age of pup at purchase, and whether the mother dog was seen interacting with her pups. The study found the prevalence of aggression and separation-related behavioral disorders is higher in dogs obtained from irresponsible breeders (Gray et al., 2016). These problems are likely due to the lack of appropriate stimulation during early life, negative experiences, minimal maternal care, or too-early separation from littermates.

Newfoundland-Specific Questions

The red flags list is merely the first screen a breeder should pass in your search for a healthy puppy. Here are some additional questions you'll want to ask the breeder:

- *How long have you been breeding?* Have you changed your practices and recommendations over the years? An experienced breeder is always learning as new information and research findings become available. A great breeder will have rethought recommendations (such as training methods or time to spay/neuter) as the veterinary and canine behavior fields have advanced.

- *How old were the grandparents and other ancestors of this litter when they died?* The likelihood of having a puppy that lives to double digits is significantly increased if there are many double-digit dogs in its pedigree. Ask the breeder about cardiac diseases, lymphoma, and other cancers in the lines. Go online yourself and look at the OFA (Orthopedic Foundation for Animals) clearances and the NCA Heath Database for health information on the ancestors of a litter you are considering.

- *What health guarantees are in the contract?* The breeder should share the Puppy Contract in advance and go over the specifics with you.

- *Can I come visit to see the mother and her puppies?* If you are building relationships with several breeders before a litter is born, it should be easy to arrange a visit to meet the dam before she has her pups. Many breeders are reluctant to allow visitors once the pups are "on the ground" until the puppies receive their first vaccines, due to the worry about infections. However, you should be able to visit a week or so before picking up a puppy. You'll want to see if the pups were raised inside the home, whether the mother is friendly and relaxed, whether the pups are playing and tussling with one another, and whether the pups are friendly and open to new people. Often, the sire is not on the premises, but you can always call the owner of the sire and ask to see photos and learn more about him.

- *Are you actively showing your dogs?* As a rule, it is best to find a breeder who is showing his or her breeding line and wants to tell you about their title accomplishments. You may also find an excellent breeder who is less interested in Conformation but wants to develop their dogs for working titles, great family pets, or therapy dogs.

- *What characteristics are you breeding for?* All breeders are looking for longevity and good temperament in their line. Breeders may also be trying to reduce a specific genetically-based problem, seeking specific physical characteristics, or breeding for an intelligent, inquisitive working dog.

- *When do you recommend spaying or neutering?* After reading the chapter on health and longevity, you may want to delay the spaying or neutering of your Newfoundland puppy to two years of age or even older. Will that work from the breeder's perspective?

- *Can I contact owners who have purchased dogs from you?* It is fine to ask for references, and you might get some good tips from current owners. All great breeders keep track of their puppies for life and are generally willing to share contact information for their happy puppy owners. On the other hand, if you have been going to local Newfoundland Club events and dog shows, you should be somewhat aware of a breeder's reputation. I knew, for example, how lucky I was to obtain my pup Willow from such an iconic breeder of distinction and would never have considered asking for references. Use your judgment on this suggestion!

- *When can we bring the puppy home?* Reputable breeders will obtain a cardiology health clearance for their puppies from a certified veterinary cardiologist. This clearance cannot occur until the pups are around 10 weeks old. In addition, puppies benefit from learning to play with their littermates, so they should not be taken away from their first home until they are 10 weeks.

- *Do you have any additional restrictions or requirements on care of your puppies?* Some breeders will require a fenced-in yard so that an electric fence is never used. Others might mandate that you feed a certain dog food. Many will require you to spay or neuter by a certain age. Some breeders will have requirements for vaccinations, tick and parasite control, veterinary care, grooming, exercise, never chaining the dog, and avoiding excessive crating or riding in the back of an open truck.

Contracts

You should expect a written contract that clearly states the ongoing relationship between the provider and your family. This written contract and the relationship will be ongoing for the life of your Newfy. The contract will stipulate guarantees and expectations of the family and provider. Reputable breeders will always specify that they will take back a dog they have bred. Sometimes the breeder will co-own the Newfy, protecting the dog for life with the stipulation that if anything arises that makes rehoming necessary, the Newfy will be returned to the breeder. Choosing the breeder is an important process. It must be someone with whom the family can work because the relationship with the breeder is for the life of the pup and beyond.

Other Giant Breeds

Some prospective owners may be looking for a giant breed but are unsure about the differences between a Newfoundland, a Great Pyrenees, and a St. Bernard. Dr. Dunphy, who has experience with all three breeds and has owned Newfoundlands and St. Bernards, offers a succinct summary:

> **66**
>
> *The Newfoundland demands to be with people. If you don't want a house dog, don't get a Newf. He is going to be at the door, wanting to come back in and not stay in the backyard. If you want a dog that likes both indoors and outdoors and likes people, get a St. Bernard. He will be happy. The Great Pyrenees are happier outside; they have their perimeter, and they patrol it. They like to have a job and are content outside.*
>
> **DR. CLYDE DUNPHY,**
> *DVM, Current Chair of the Newfoundland*
> *Club of American Charitable Trust*
>
> **99**

Consider a Rescue, Older Dog, or Shelter Dog

Many regional Newfoundland clubs have active rescue committees. Preliminary data suggest that the number of dogs put through rescue is increasing. People surrender Newfoundlands for differing reasons. The NCA and regional clubs are great resources for finding a rescue. These groups provide initial veterinary care and assess what placement is in the best interest of the Newfy and its prospective family. With any Newfy, and especially for a rescue Newfy, appropriate placement is paramount for all to thrive. You may also want to check with your local shelter as a Newfy or Newf-mix may be there waiting to join your family. Shelters and rescue organizations will require that you share detailed information about your lifestyle and may require home inspections. These organizations work hard to ensure that dogs are placed in appropriate homes so that they are not given up again.

Because Newfs are generally sweet and docile, a rescue Newf is unlikely to be aggressive with people or other dogs. The rescue may be ill-trained, and that can be a challenge in a big dog, but an adult dog can be retrained. Learn what motivates your adult Newf. Is it treats? Praise? Being patted a certain way? An adult dog that has not been well socialized might benefit from an Adult Obedience class or from private sessions with a trainer. See the chapter on training for some suggestions for training adult dogs.

We have seen an increase in the number of dogs going into rescue. They get a cute puppy for the kids, but they do not realize the amount of training needed to be a good canine citizen. The rescues are not bad dogs; they just are rambunctious and don't have good manners. We still see a fair number of dogs given up to rescue because of a divorce, a change in the family situation, or a change in the health of a family member. The third reason may be the cost of health care for Newfs. We see dogs surrendered to rescue for that reason and have some programs like the Barrister Fund to help with the funding of veterinary treatment.

DR. CLYDE DUNPHY

Advice about Adopting an Older Dog

A Bernese Mountain Dog rescue group offers this advice about adopting an older dog:

"An older puppy or mature dog can be a good alternative, especially for households where the family pet may have to spend much of the day unsupervised. Older dogs may be available for several reasons. Breeders often hold a puppy until they can determine its show/breeding potential; a bitch that has been bred once or twice may be retired. Circumstances change. Someone may have to give up a much-loved pet, or an unruly dog could be taken into a rescue program. These dogs are usually housetrained, may know some cues, and have formed many behavior patterns. Rescue advocates say that adopted dogs take three days to decompress, three days to understand your household routines, and three months to feel at home. Give your adopted dog a chance to adjust."

Photo Courtesy of Jessica Hoffman

> "
>
> *Henry was a beautiful much-loved pup who was only with his new family one week when his new Human Dad suffered a massive heart attack and passed. His new Mom was already in compromised health and could not care for him, breaking her heart a second time when she realized the puppy her husband and she looked forward to for so long would not be able to stay with her. Our stepping in took place within 24 hours. The breeder was involved but lived across the country. We fostered Henry and became very close with the pup. So did our intact male, Wyley, who took Henry in as if he was his own. It brought me to tears to experience the GENTLE GIANT in our boy! I will never forget the 21 days we all spent together. The breeder had already contacted the next family in line for one of her pups, and they were thrilled but needed time to travel and get him. We drove from Illinois to Indiana to deliver Henry to another volunteer who traveled to Ohio for the last leg of his forever home delivery.*
>
> CISSY SULLIVAN
> *Newfoundland Owner and Photographer*
>
> "

Don't hesitate to take a good-natured adult Newfoundland into your home. Although the dog may be confused at first, patience, consistency, and reassurance are key. The dog's self-confidence will return, and it will adapt readily to your routine. A few breeder/rescue tips on adopting an older dog:

- Learn all you can about the dog you are considering and determine if it will fit into your lifestyle.

- Learn about the dog's habits, diet, and history. If this is not available, perhaps you could take the dog for a week for observation.

- Be sure all family members meet the dog before it is adopted and they agree that this is the right decision. It is best to acquire the older dog when you can be at home with it full time for the first few days so the dog can learn what is expected of it, where it is to relieve itself, when meals will be served, etc.

*Photo Courtesy
of Cissy Sullivan*

Consider a Newf from a Shelter

This is an area where people of goodwill may disagree, but here are a few pros and cons you should consider in your decision about a getting a shelter dog versus buying from a reputable breeder:

PROS

- You are saving a dog's life and giving it a second chance for a happy life.
- You are helping a shelter by making room for a new dog and supporting its important humane mission. Although the pandemic significantly increased the number of dogs adopted from shelters, more than 300,000 dogs were euthanized in 2020 in the United States.
- You might avoid some of the work of raising a puppy, and your new dog may already be partially trained.
- You will pay less for your new Newf.
- By going to a shelter or rescue, you are not inadvertently supporting the puppy mill/cruel pet trade.
- You'll get basic information about the dog you adopt its likes and dislikes.

CONS

- The dog has a history and, as a result, might have behavior issues such as separation anxiety or aggression.
- You'll fill out a lot of paperwork before you get your dog.
- Socialization during the critical puppy phase may have been inadequate, so you are more likely to discover behavioral issues.
- It may be hard to find a Newf or Newf mix in a shelter.

Each dog is different, and each household is different, so you'll want to weigh the options when you consider adopting a shelter Newf.

Mixed-Breed Crosses

And what about mixed breeds like the Newfoundland poodle? Crossbreeding *might possibly* produce puppies with desirable traits such as hypoallergenic fur or longevity that appeal to some owners. The disadvantages of crossbreed mixes stem from a lack of a national organization like

Photo Courtesy of Heidi Peterson

Photo Courtesy of Cathy Derench

the Newfoundland Club of America to vet breeders, maintain health data-bases, and establish standards. At the same time, the gentle temperament and personality that make Newfs so special might get lost along the way; remember the Moscow Water Dog from the first chapter. It is difficult to generalize, but "designer dog" breeders could possibly be puppy mills out to make money from the high demand for such dogs. You should be sure to carefully check out a breeder if you're considering a mixed-breed cross.

> *We were alerted by a breeder about the plight of four-year-old Riley, who was brought into rescue very pregnant and about to give birth. Riley was well taken care of by her family but had been impregnated by another Newfoundland in the house. We agreed to take her into rescue and help with the puppies, assuring the family that although they had to sign over ownership so That Newfoundland Place could approve veterinary care, we would do our best to return Riley to the family. She gave birth to 9 puppies by c-section, and it was a joy to see those purebred puppies thrive and find forever homes across the country. Riley, who was spayed, was returned to the family after they agreed to neuter their other dog. Everyone was thrilled with the outcome.*
>
> **CATHY DERENCH**
> *That Newfoundland Place*

CHAPTER 4

Preparations for Pup

Puppy proofing, planning, and purchasing are key elements of preparing for your new pup. Once you've identified when you'll be picking up your new Newf, prepare for her arrival by clearing your calendar to ease her transition to your home, puppy-proofing your home, and purchasing the supplies you will need to care for the newest family member. You'll likely want to modify aspects of your home to make it dog-friendly, with particular attention to fencing in the backyard and to floor surfaces that are nonslip for a growing Newfoundland. You'll need a good vacuum cleaner and may want to get large cloth coverings for your furniture.

Floors, Balconies, and Stairs

Photo Courtesy of Katie Dolan

Newfoundlands grow quickly and mature slowly. They can be very clumsy and should avoid walking on slippery surfaces while developing. Placing an area rug over a tile or hardwood floor will give your puppy more stability and help avoid slips and falls that could damage a developing skeletal system. Stair treads are also a good idea. And be sure to block off open balconies and high areas from which a puppy might fall. Indoor gates are helpful to restrict

Photo Courtesy of Katie Dolan

the puppy to parts of the home and to prevent her from trying to navigate steep stairs before she is able. (Pups develop depth perception at about six months of age. Pups can ascend stairs at an early age, but descending can cause broken limbs.)

Fencing and Water Bodies

Although a Newfoundland can thrive and be happy in an apartment or condo, if its owner is attentive to the dog's need for outdoor exercise, a fenced yard is best for your dog's health and safety. The fence should be at least five feet high; many recommend six feet for a Newfoundland. Electric fencing is not a good option for a Newfoundland because the collar doesn't work well with the dog's thick coat of hair, and dogs often run through electric fences. Many Newfoundland breeders will not sell you a puppy unless you agree not to use an electric fence. A dog should never be chained or tied outside where it would be vulnerable to predators. Newfs are people-pets and should never be chained.

If you have an outdoor pool, pond, or lake, be sure to have it fenced off from where the dog might be spending time. Even though Newfs are generally good swimmers, your pup needs to learn to swim first and may also not know how to get out of a pool safely. A life jacket is used by many owners to help teach young pups how to swim. Be especially aware of frozen bodies of water and the risk of a dog falling through the ice in the wintertime.

Puppy-Proofing

Dog/puppy-proofing your home is key to safety, peace of mind, and avoiding unnecessary trips for veterinary care. A puppy will chew and cause damage to your home if left unattended. Poisonous plants should be removed to protect your new addition. Be particularly careful about power cords. The puppy-proofing process should include a "final inspection," where you crawl around and look from a lower angle. Remember that your Newf will grow, so items that cannot be reached by a puppy will soon become accessible. Unlike humans, who must develop a taste for new foods, dogs are willing to try anything that might be food.

Newfoundlands are great at finding extra food. My Newf Bella consistently proved the Polish proverb, "The dog kennel is no place to store a sausage." She jumped on counters and helped herself to pies, roasts, and bananas. She rummaged in the garbage bins mounted on a circular lazy Susan corner contraption. After installing special locks, we heard thumps in the night as she pushed on the garbage can cabinet doors with her snout. Another time, with skills rivaling Houdini, Bella opened a zipped-closed, soft ice chest stored outdoors, smelling frozen lamb stew. She wrestled with the Tupperware container in our backyard. The container skittered 10 feet across the hard-packed March snow and finally came to rest in a patch of dirt. After a tussle, I regained possession of the well-licked stew.

When we designed our new home here in Colorado, we installed an extra-high kitchen island (54 inches tall) and smugly thought we'd finally found a solution to Bella's food thievery. However, we came into the kitchen and found Bella precariously balancing on a swivel chair, with her forepaws on the chair back and her snout in the middle of a plate of cheese on the high island. In hindsight, I should have been more consistent about not giving her human foods, trained her more effectively, and fed her in a location far from the kitchen.

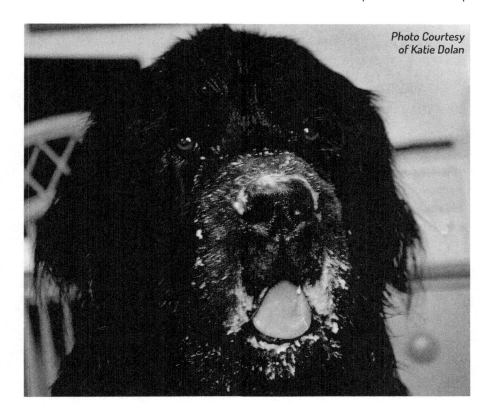

Photo Courtesy of Katie Dolan

A helpful reminder: a large Newf will gobble down partially chewed corncobs and risk getting a dangerous bowel obstruction. Be sure to put trash away safely and pay attention to corncobs and debris at firepits or cook fireplaces in the woods or at the beach.

The American Veterinary Medicine Association offers a comprehensive brochure about "Pet Hazards In Your Home And Garden" (www.avma.org). It has been adapted below, with a particular emphasis on Newfoundlands.

Hazards in the Kitchen

Garbage Cans: One of the biggest sources of stolen foods for our Newfoundlands has always been kitchen garbage cans. We've learned from experience and now put our trash and recycling cans in a roll-out cabinet, so the garbage is always behind closed doors. The stand-alone garbage cans, even with secure tops, can be knocked over by an inquisitive Newf.

Foods: Some favorite human foods are potentially deadly to Newfoundlands and other dogs. These items include coffee grounds, fatty foods, tea, chocolate, avocado, salt, macadamia nuts, alcohol, yeast dough, grapes/raisins, onions, garlic, and any food products containing xylitol (an artificial sweetener in chewing gum and some peanut butters). Dark chocolate has more cacao and so is more problematic than milk chocolate. A full-grown Newfoundland, because of its weight, would have to consume over a pound of chocolate to cause a problem. This could happen if the dog gets into Halloween candy or into a guest's suitcase where chocolate hostess gifts might be stored. In addition, be sure guest handbags, which may have gum with xylitol, are always put in a secure place.

Cleaning Products: Store cleaning products in a secure cabinet out of the reach of pets and keep them in their original packaging or in a clearly labeled and tightly sealed container. Because Newfoundlands are large, you may want to install kid-proof mechanisms on cabinets where cleaning products are stored.

Insecticides/Rodenticides: Read and follow label instructions before using any type of pesticide in your pet's environment. It is important to place any poison in areas completely inaccessible to pets. Better yet, do not use rodenticides—they wreak havoc on birds and other wildlife that eat the poisoned rodents. See https://www.raptorsarethesolution.org website for wildlife-safe alternatives for rodent control.

Hazards in the Bathroom

Medications: Some human medications can make pets sick. For example, the active ingredient in Advil almost did not make it to human clinical trials because it was so toxic to dogs. Never give your pet any medication, including over-the-counter medications, unless directed by your veterinarian. Medicines should be tightly closed and stored securely and away from pets.

Cleaning Products: Be careful when using toilet bowl cleaner as Newfs think the toilet is the perfect height for a water fountain and will be tempted to drink from it.

Soaps and Sundries: If ingested, these can cause stomach upset. My Newfoundlands have always been attracted to shaving cream and like to steal and chew on soap bars.

Hazards in the Living Room

Potpourri: Liquid potpourri products contain ingredients that can cause oral ulcerations and other problems in pets.

Mothballs: A single mothball can sicken a dog. The main ingredient, naphthalene, can cause digestive tract irritation, liver, kidney, blood cell damage, swelling of the brain tissues, seizures, coma, respiratory tract damage (if inhaled), and death (if ingested). Tobacco products, pennies (those minted after 1982 contain zinc), and alkaline batteries (like those in your remote controls) can also be hazardous if ingested.

Drugs: Drugs, including marijuana, can pose life-threatening risks to pets. Notify your veterinarian immediately if you suspect your pet has ingested a narcotic substance.

Hazards in the Garage and Yard

Herbicides, Antifreeze, Paints, and Solvents: These are all dangerous for pets.

Toxic plants: A surprising number of plants are toxic, so check the American Veterinary Medicine Association brochure Pet hazards in your home and garden: www.avma.org for a comprehensive list of plants and greenery that put your pet at risk.

On the other hand, many popular flowers and plants are safe for dogs, including sunflowers, African violets, snapdragons, orchids, roses, garden marigolds, pansies, petunias, zinnias, and Gerber daisies.

Garbage Cans: Again, garbage cans are very tempting for a Newfoundland with a good nose for decomposing foods.

Newfoundland Puppy/Dog Shopping List

In addition to getting your home ready for its new resident, you'll want to have some key items on hand for the dog's arrival. Before you pick up your new puppy or dog, spend time purchasing the items you will need to safely care for your pet. And be sure to stay away from items that could injure your dog. (The list was adapted from information provided by my friend, Linda Seaver, a Bernese Mountain Dog breeder.)

Crates/Exercise Pens

For traveling, crate training, and general puppy management, you'll want at least one crate. The largest crates do not necessarily fit into all cars, so check the height of your vehicle and measure where you will put any crate. You might want to have a smaller collapsible crate for car rides as the puppy grows, as well as a larger crate that can be divided into smaller sizes for initial housetraining.

A fleece crate pad may comfort your pup and be easy to throw into the wash, but many Newf owners find that their dogs prefer the coolness of a vinyl crate pad. An Extra-Large sized crate from Midwest cages with a divider panel will work from puppyhood to adult-sized Newfoundland. You'll also want to look at wooden gates to separate various parts of your home. You might also consider an exercise pen for use both indoors and out. Just as with a human baby, these exercise pens can keep you pup safe while you do other things around the house or garden.

Food and Bowls

It is best to initially feed whatever the breeder has been giving the puppy or whatever the rescue group has been feeding your new dog. See the nutrition chapter for a full discussion of options. In addition, it is a good idea to have some white rice or canned pumpkin on hand in case the new arrival gets an upset stomach. You'll want to have at least two bowls—one for food and one for water. Both should be washed with soap and water daily. To store leftover dog food, use only glass or commercial food-grade plastic, as chemicals in lesser-grade plastic can become reactive and leach into food.

Harnesses, Collars, and Leashes

Your Newfoundland puppy will be growing four pounds per week, so plan to increase the sizes of her collars over time. A ThunderLeash, which hooks to the collar and then can be wrapped around the puppy and secured into a harness, will work as your dog grows. You'll also want to purchase several teaching leads. One leash should be six feet long for around the house, walks and obedience classes, and the other should be a longer line for teaching a reliable recall. You'll be happy to have a few slip leads (which go over the dog's head as a collar/leash) for short trips from the house to the car, and it's good to have one to leave in your car.

Newfoundlands, especially dogs that may be used for draft work, will associate a harness with using their strong chest to pull an object. That is why many Newfoundland owners suggest using a snug collar and a slip leash placed high enough on the dog's neck (like a halter on a horse) to control its head and rest right behind the ears.

Choke chains, and especially prong collars, have been found to cause damage to the esophagus or trachea. A dog's spine, thyroid, and eyes can be negatively affected. Pressure from an inappropriately placed collar can contribute to glaucoma. A 2006 study conducted by a veterinary ophthalmologist "showed an increase in intraocular pressure" in dogs while pulling on a collar. In addition, a pup pulling its owner toward other dogs may associate the pain from a prong collar with the sight of dogs, potentially leading to aggressiveness. Although some Newf owners use choke chains and prong collars in specific and limited situations for safety, many do not want to take the risk of injuring their dog.

Photo Courtesy of Katie Dolan

Grooming Tools and Shampoo

You'll want to invest in dog shampoo and some grooming tools so your puppy gets used to being groomed from a young age. At a minimum, you'll want a brush with one-inch prongs with ball pins and a Mars Coat King for pulling out undercoat, trimming ears, dematting, and untangling. See the grooming chapter for more on suggested tools.

Toys

Newfoundlands have a need to chew and powerful jaws that can chew through seemingly indestructible plastic and hard rubber items. Choose toys wisely and always supervise him while he enjoys his chew toys. As your puppy gets older, his jaws will get stronger. Providing a variety of toys will hopefully make your furniture less appealing. Have a supply of larger-sized

*Photo Courtesy
of Heidi Peterson*

Puppy Kongs to fill with kibble, yogurt, cheese, peanut butter, or biscuits. Keep one in the freezer for your teething puppy. These will entertain him and hopefully reduce inappropriate chewing and biting. Try to get toys that appeal to you, as your puppy will play with anything. Fake lambskin babies are great and can be thrown in the washer. Jolly Balls and Indestructible Balls are super, but always get two, so you can play chase without playing keep away. You may also want to purchase Katie's Brand bumpers, which are a good size for your pup to carry around prior to water rescue work.

Miscellaneous and Future Purchases to Consider

You might purchase a treat pouch; the one by Karen Pryor/Terry Ryan comes highly recommended. Other items you'll want to have on hand include tomato juice to remedy skunk odor and a stain and odor remover for cleaning up after accidents. Over time, consider a cooling mat for your Newf to relax on during warm weather. You'll also want to consider a ramp or steps for easy Newf access to your car and a car safety harness. See details in the chapter on traveling with your Newf.

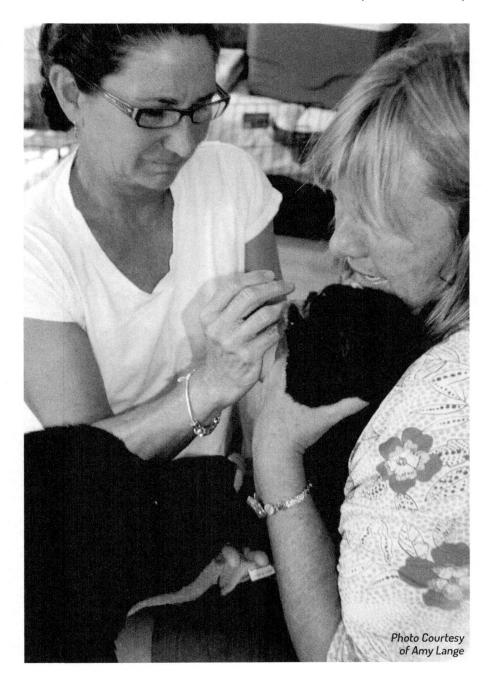

*Photo Courtesy
of Amy Lange*

Items To Avoid

NO NYLABONES!!!!! One pup I know managed to retain a cup of chewed plastic in her stomach for three months. Toys with braided colored string and toys with button eyes can be dangerous if swallowed. Rawhide bones and pig ears should also be avoided because they can get stuck in the trachea, puncture the intestines, and are treated with formaldehyde. (Use frozen beef or bison bone marrow bones instead. I get the larger size to avoid any chance that my Newfs will try to swallow the bones.) Avoid all cooked bones, as they can splinter and cause damage.

Choosing a Veterinarian

Picking a veterinarian experienced in the care of Newfs or giant breed dogs is ideal. The best resources for referral are members of the regional Newfoundland club and neighbors with Newfs. You may want to meet a few veterinarians before you select one where the chemistry between you is good. A veterinarian experienced with the breed will be able to give you informed advice about vaccines, routine care, preventing and treating parasites, common Newfy diseases, managing weight, and appropriate timing for spaying and neutering, as well as a gastropexy to prevent bloat. You may also want to consider a veterinarian with integrative health expertise and training.

Most breeders will suggest you bring your new puppy to the veterinarian within a few days of bringing the puppy home so that everyone agrees the new arrival is healthy. Try to model calmness at the veterinarian's office. A recent study of dogs and their owners at veterinary appointments shows a link between dog and owner behaviors: when owners attend an examination, their negative behaviors intensify the signs of anxiety in their dogs. The more that dogs display stress-related behaviors, the more they establish eye contact with their owners, suggesting that dogs seek information and reassurance from their owners.

Preparing Other Pets in the Household

In general, Newfs are friendly with other household pets. There are even stories of Newfoundlands befriending rabbits and other wild animals. For household cats, an escape tower will give the feline a place to get away from a friendly Newf. You might also want to expose any other household pets to a Newfy-scented blanket before the real dog arrives in the household.

Photo Courtesy
of The Zimmerman Collection
Peter Moran

Some veterinarians recommend a "preparing the pets" physical examination appointment for cats and dogs already in the household. The
appointment is an opportunity to discuss canine and feline body language,
so owners know to look for signs of stress. To educate children about
these signs, there's a board game that teaches canine body language.
Dog-appeasing pheromones may also be prescribed to ease the new pet
introductions. In addition, household pets should be desensitized to being
confined in safe, secure spaces before the new Newf arrives.

CHAPTER 5

Homecoming and Housetraining

"

"Professor Barney" came from a very highly regarded breeder in Saskatchewan. His homecoming at eleven weeks of age was carefully handled, which resulted in immediate bonding with us, his new owners. Our senior Newf, Hannah, came along for the trip.

At eleven weeks old, Barney endured a rather scary flight to Ontario, where we first met. There was a packet of food taped to his travel crate, and the breeder told me, "Whoever feeds him first will be his lifelong buddy." She was so right about that. I fed him little bits through the crate on the drive to Pennsylvania, and the die was cast.

My schedule was cleared for the next week, and Barney settled in nicely with us, his new friend Hannah, and even our two cats. How you handle homecoming means everything to your new best friend and your life together. We put Barney's crate right next to our bed with the door open. Eventually, we moved the crate to the dining room, and he started following Hannah's lead. We also fed both dogs in their separate crates. Barney became a wonderful therapy dog and participated in water rescue with great vigor.

KAREN STEINROCK
Newfoundland owner

"

Patience, puppy-proofing, and potty training are key words for this exciting phase with your new dog. Get ready to fall in love with your cute companion. Many Newf owners are besotted. Our brains and hormones are genetically engineered to want to care for and nurture human babies and, by extension, a young animal with big eyes, a round head, a fuzzy body, and an

Photo Courtesy of Karen Steinrock

infant-like appearance. Konrad Lorenz, the Nobel prize–winning ethologist and zoologist, coined the term "the baby schema effect."

Develop a Plan

The new addition will bring new responsibilities and routines. Talk with all family members to decide the safe places (a crate or closed-off room) for your puppy. Develop a schedule for feeding, walking, and getting up in the middle of the night with the new dog. Try to clear your calendar to be around so you can help ease your new dog's transition to your home. Put the plan in writing so everyone remembers who is supposed to do what and when. Otherwise, your new pup might get too many dinners and no breakfast! You'll also want to agree on who is the primary person to train the pup, although everyone should be using the same cues for basic obedience training. Get young children engaged in the planning by asking them to draw images of the rules or by creating a Puppy Calendar with assigned roles and stars for tasks completed. Explain the pup is still a baby with very specific needs: young children must let the pup sleep when it is in its crate, learn to play with a puppy without mauling it, and try to avoid running away from the pup. Children can frighten puppies because they don't have the self-control to move slowly and quietly. All dogs are drawn to calm people who move slowly and don't crowd them.

50

Photo Courtesy
of Katie Dolan

Picking Up Pup

Plan your trip so that you have some time to get to know the breeder or rescue organizer, ask any questions you may have, and go over and sign the contract and other papers. Ideally, pick up the puppy in the middle of the day, so you have time to get acquainted while everyone is fresh. Remember, the day is a beginning for you and your family but an ending for the breeder. Your puppy has been lovingly raised by the breeder's family. They need to say goodbye and are likely feeling emotional about the departure.

Supplies you will want to bring when you pick up your puppy from the breeder include a crate, an empty water jug to fill with water at the breeder's home, treats, and a toy for the crate. In addition, bring a toy or blanket to the pick-up. Rub it on the other pups and the mom, then keep it with the pup when you bring her home. You may also want to bring a small collar and leash in case you need them for stops along the way home.

Although it is very tempting to cuddle a puppy on a passenger's lap, it is safest to put her in a secure crate for the ride home. Be sure to pull over for potty breaks every hour. Try to find quiet rest-stop locations where the pup will not be exposed to other dogs and their germs. When we were driving young Willow home from Tennessee to Rhode Island, we tried to find parks and natural areas for our stops. Plug in "parks nearby" on your GPS map, and some nice puppy spots might pop up.

Let your pup rest. Play soothing music if that seems to help. Your pup may be frightened by the car ride and new people; act calmly and communicate by your voice and gestures that all will be well. Speak gently and softly. Let your puppy sleep.

When you arrive home, introduce the puppy to any other dogs in the household in a neutral space outdoors if possible. Keep everyone on a leash and let the sniffing begin. Supervise this interaction closely. Older dogs are generally patient with puppies, even when young dogs have not yet learned the finer social graces of dog greetings. Even if the initial meeting goes smoothly, watch for signs of excitability. Research suggests that excitement is the most common trigger for fighting among dogs in the same household, followed by food and toys. Reward good behaviors between the animals.

Photo Courtesy of Katie Dolan

Separate the newcomer from other pets when unsupervised and provide for other pets to get regular breaks from the puppy.

Blue and Willow are tussling more frequently as she gets older. He usually rolls over on his back with his paws in the air while she feints and charges around him, barking. We can tell when he is ready for a break. The pitch of his bark changes. I read that research shows household dogs typically prefer to be within 23 inches of each other, and I notice that Willow typically curls up about two feet away from Blue on either the cool bathroom floor or the soft dog couch by the fireplace. It's good to know that they are simply following patterns seen in other multi-dog homes.

First Night

Play with the puppy. Give her water from the breeder's home and serve her the food she's been eating at the same time she usually eats. If you are crate training, place the crate near your bed. Put toys and the towel that smells of her littermates in the crate. Prepare yourself for interrupted sleep and for a middle-of-the-night potty-break and an early morning wake-up. Be patient and soothing when the pup whines, as she misses the warm comfort, sounds, and smells of her littermates. Most puppies miss their mother and

Photo Courtesy
of Jen Costello

littermates for the first few days. With all that puppy fur, having a fan blow on the pup might help.

>
>
> *A Newf puppy is like a baby. It will need to be near or with humans. It has left its mother and littermates, so the adjustment is huge. A crate set up in the bedroom works great! This will allow the Newf to be close to its humans and can signal when it is time to go outdoors. Potty breaks are very frequent.*
>
> AMY CULVER DAVIS
> *Birchbark Newfoundlands*

Crate Training

Most breeders recommend a crate for housetraining, to keep your puppy safe, and to provide a comfortable, familiar place for resting. Make the crate a fun experience, and never use the crate as a form of punishment. Dogs sleep 17 hours a day, and most love sleeping in their crate. Free-rein training is an alternative to crate training that some owners prefer. However, there will be situations in your dog's life when she will need to be in a crate: for safe travel in a car, at the veterinarian, or when being groomed. So, it is important to get your pup comfortable with a crate.

Tips on Crate Training:

- Make the crate his comfy and inviting home.
- Use a vinyl or fleece crate pad for comfort. (Newfs generally prefer a cooler surface.)
- Let the pup sniff around and explore his new crate. Add some treats and let him get used to the new space and settle in. Leave the door ajar so he can go in and out. (It is likely his breeder had small crates in the Puppy play area at his first home.)
- Put your pup in his crate for short 10-minute stints when he is already worn out. Gradually increase the amount of time the pup is asked to stay in his crate.
- The crate should be near his people, preferably by your bed.
- A top over the crate can make it feel more like a den and help the pup settle down.

- Provide an interesting toy or food treat so he associates the crate with great things.
- Feed him meals in his crate.
- Use a hanging bucket to provide water without spillage.
- Maintain a regular feeding schedule.
- Leave the crate door open when the pup is out and about so he can retreat to it on his own.
- Walk him before bedtime, then put him in his crate when he is tired. Calmly talk to and reassure him when he whimpers. At first, you'll have to let him out to relieve himself every few hours at night.
- You might want to keep a housetraining log to record and evaluate whether accidents are becoming less frequent. Your log should include the schedule, what was done and when (urination and defecation), and note any accident (time and location).
- Consider using a second crate so that your pup can be near the action during the day and by your bedside at night. You can also move a crate around to accomplish the same thing.

Free-rein training, in which the dog is allowed to be in a safe, puppy-proofed part of the house with no crating, has worked well with my Newfs. We closed off two rooms and carefully puppy-proofed the area. We can safely leave the dogs in this area when we go out. I sometimes put Willow, our new pup, in a crate in the car to practice so she will not be upset while at the groomer or veterinarian. Free-rein housetraining for Willow makes sense because we have a dog door leading to a safe, grass-covered outside deck. We also have a ten-year-old, very patient Newf. The puppy quickly learned how to use the dog door and emulated our older dog, so her early housetraining at the breeder's home was reinforced. Because we live in mountain lion country, the outside deck is on the second floor, out of reach for a leaping cougar.

Housetraining

Among wild canids, keeping the den clean is an important way to remain inconspicuous where other predators lurk. This same instinct helps when housebreaking a puppy. Horses, monkeys, and cattle cannot be housebroken because they do not have this "clean den" instinct.

Schedule: Having a consistent schedule for feeding and walking your pup will help his digestive system get on a regular schedule too. Your Newf will need to go outside as soon as he awakes, finishes eating or drinking, or finishes playing. Pups under 20–30 weeks old will need to urinate every hour while they are awake and even more frequently if they are playing. (Adult dogs should be let out every six to eight hours). In general, because of their size, Newfoundlands are easy to housetrain. Our dogs have been trained by 4-5 months, with perhaps an accident occasionally. If you catch your pup in the early phase of squatting, you can sometimes say a firm "No" and take her immediately to the designated spot for relieving herself. If your puppy is getting ready to defecate, a relocation is not likely to work.

No Punishment: Never push his nose into the mess: your pup will not understand, and your relationship with him may suffer. A sensitive Newf who is harshly corrected for having an accident may think that elimination is a bad thing. In one study, owners giving their dogs up at shelters were asked to respond to the statement, "It is helpful to rub the dog's nose in her mess when she soils in the house." Almost one-third (31.8%) said they believed that was true, and another 11% said they were "not sure." The authors of the study noted that there was "room for improvement" in educating dog owners about appropriate housetraining methods. As we will see in the training chapter, a growing body of research confirms that negative reinforcement is not as effective as positive training methods.

Consistency and Praise: Take your dog outside to the same spot where the family wants him to perform his bodily functions. Choose a cue like "Go Potty," and repeat it each time the Newfy is where he is expected to urinate or defecate. When the pup is in the process of doing the task, say, "Good, Go Potty," and as soon as he finishes, reward him immediately with a high-value treat. Pups easily get distracted by the wonderful smells outdoors and may forget to get down to business, so you'll need to pay attention to their actions (or inaction).

Gradual Free-Rein: Many new dog owners move too quickly to allowing their housetrained (or mostly housetrained) Newfs to have free-rein of the house. The "clean den" instinct generally applies to parts of the home used regularly by people and dogs. Remote parts of the house (irregularly used bedrooms, study areas, etc.) may be viewed by a dog as outside of its "home" and thus a place to urinate or mark its territory. We always close bedroom doors, so these remote areas are less tempting for our young dog.

Older Dogs: When housetraining or retraining an older dog, use the same techniques outlined above.

Regression: If a dog regresses and begins to eliminate in the house, check with your veterinarian and confirm that there is not an underlying medical issue. A dog with a urinary tract infection (common among female

Newfoundlands) will have to urinate very frequently and may make a mistake. Fortunately, the antibiotics work quickly. Separation Anxiety can also cause a dog to regress.

Sleep

Give your puppy plenty of opportunities to snooze. Dog cognition expert Alexandra Horowitz and her colleagues have found dogs remember a learned behavior (touching a hand with the nose) better after a period of sleep. The dogs that slept after learning the behavior were faster and more accurate in retention.

Photo Courtesy
of Katie Dolan

Taking Your Leave

After the puppy has adjusted to his new home and family, practice the routine of leaving. Grab your car keys, put on your coat, and exit the house. Then turn around and come back inside within a short period of time. Do this several times so your pup gets used to the routine of your departures.

Puppy Zoomies

My Willow, at age seven months, loves getting the puppy zoomies. She runs in circles with abandon. We must be careful to let her run and zoom in a safe space. We are currently in early spring thaw, with piles of soft snow and, even worse, crusty snow on top of old snow, creating the possibility of post-holing. I must keep her leashed so she doesn't make flying joyous leaps off the snowbanks.

As the graphic from the Newfoundland Club of America illustrates, the femur and other long bones of a Newfoundland are still growing at one year of age, while the pelvis continues to grow in the dog's second year. Damage to the ligaments and bones at a young age can become serious arthritis as the dog ages. If you have a young Newfoundland, you need to be your dog's advocate because she has no sense of self-preservation. Your puppy is growing at an exponential rate, and even if she does not show any pain or discomfort, repeated high-impact activity can cause long-term joint issues. Continued minor muscle and growth plate strains can make your dog vulnerable to future injuries, including sprains, ligament tears, and more. See the chapter on exercising your Newf for further information.

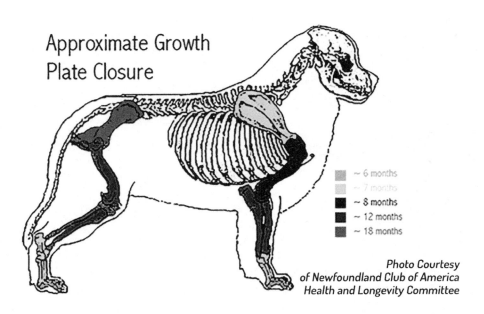

Approximate Growth Plate Closure

~ 6 months
~ 7 months
~ 8 months
~ 12 months
~ 18 months

Photo Courtesy of Newfoundland Club of America Health and Longevity Committee

CHAPTER 6
Training Your Newfoundland

> "
>
> *I ask you to sponge your mind clear of prejudice...in a word, make yourself a puppy again, with all that implies of receptivity and hospitable welcome to any new thing.*
>
> MARK TWAIN
> from "Newfoundland Smith's Letters from a Dog to Another Dog Explaining and Accounting for Man"
>
> "

Consistency. Positive reinforcement. Fun. Manage distractions. These are your cues for enjoyably and effectively training your dog. Because Newfoundlands grow into such large animals that can jump up on people or knock someone down in their exuberance, having an untrained dog can be dangerous. Poor behavior is the number one reason why dogs are surrendered to shelters. It is also important to keep training your dog for her entire life.

Key Considerations

Various dog obedience methods have been used over the years, but a growing collection of research suggests consistent training done with positive reinforcement is most effective. Earlier training methods focusing on dominance and pack hierarchy were based on observations of unrelated wolves in a confined area. Recent studies of wolves in natural packs suggest friendly interactions in relationships akin to a family are the norm, with adults guiding the group. For a domestic dog, the relationship with its human is like the attachment between a child and its mother. Both dog and human exhibit physiological responses, including lower stress hormones and higher oxytocin levels, during close interactions. (See Recent Research on Rover box)

Newfs respond best to a positive, reward-based training approach. If you are planning to do water rescue, therapy dog, carting, or other work, your pup will need strong basic skills and training. The AKC Star Puppy and Canine Good Citizen (CGC) cer-tifications are great places to teach good manners and response to basic cues. Your dog should respect you but never fear you. This is import-ant with Newfs, given their high sensitivity level. Many Newf owners incorporate cross-training (using both verbal and visual cues) in their dogs' training. When you give a verbal cue, simultaneously use a gesture so your dog gets familiar with both ways of understanding you. This method is helpful if your dog becomes deaf as he ages or is in a noisy situation where only visual cues can be seen.

Photo Courtesy of Katie Dolan

Demeanor and Body Language

Calm, quiet humans are preferred by most dogs, who tend to be appre-hensive of people who are noisy, make sudden movements, or tower over them. Try not to stare into a dog's eyes when you first meet him; it is a sign of aggression among wild canids and with some dogs. Remember to be a calm-ing influence when your dog meets other dogs or is in stressful situations.

"

Always make outings and introductions positive. Have fun with lots of treats and praise. If you make sure that your Newf is trained (no pulling on a leash and sits when asked), most introductions to oth-er well-behaved dogs are rarely an issue. In other words, make sure you have a well-behaved and trained Newf beginning from the mo-ment you get your new puppy. Puppy school is highly recommend-ed, as well as a course in basic obedience. Organized classes are best for distractions when training.

CECE GUYATT
Trinity Cove Newfoundlands

"

RECENT RESEARCH ON ROVER

A recently published study of 92 dogs enrolled in training schools with different teaching methods firmly confirmed dogs learned a new skill faster when a reward-based training is used. With more aversive training (shock collars, pinch collars), dogs exhibited higher stress levels, both during the training session and at home. (Viera de Castro et al. "Does Training Method Matter: Evidence for the Negative Impact of Aversive-based Methods on Companion Dog Welfare." PLoS One, December 2020).

A review of YouTube videos of trainers teaching dogs to lie down assessed the "dogmanship" of the humans and found they were highly attuned to the distractions a dog faces. It also found dogs generally look away after receiving a food treat, capturing a dog's attention is time-sensitive, and non-speech vocalizations (i.e., "hey") elicit a quicker response than traditional speech commands. (Elyssa Payne et al. "DogTube: An Examination of Dogmanship Online." Journal of Veterinary Behavior, October 2016).

Evidence-based training (detailed observational studies of humans and dogs interacting) suggests what is rewarding may depend on the task being learned and the individual dog. Obedience for not chewing objects is greater when the dog is given a substitute object to chew. Obedience for "Give" or "Leave It" is higher when the dog is trained with play as a reward, while "heel" is greater for dogs using praise as a reward. I've seen this in Willow. When she is playing with the flirt pole, she will readily "leave it" so play can resume as quickly as possible. Recent research has assessed multiple factors in human-animal interaction, including eye contact, high-pitched vocal cues, body position of the human, and proximity, to understand how dogs learn.

Smaller dogs are generally less obedient and are more likely to be fearful and aggressive. The owners of smaller dogs are less likely to engage in consistent training and are more likely to be tolerant of aggression (Christine Arhant et al. Behavior of Smaller and Larger Dogs. 2010).

Dogs attending classes using aversive training methods were more likely to be pessimistic in a cognitive test involving food located in a bowl on the right but not in a bowl on the left; then, the bowls were moved to a central location. The results suggest that dogs trained with aversive techniques have a decreased expectation of reward and a longer-term negative mood state. (Rachel Casey et al. "Dogs Are More Pessimistic if Their Owners Use Two or More Aversive Training Methods." Scientific Reports, 2021).

Tone and Gender

Dogs generally respond more readily to higher-pitched voices with softer tones. A study conducted in the United Kingdom found canines loved high-pitched baby talk combined with dog-related speech, like adults talking to human babies. My children often complain about my "speaking canine," which makes our dogs pay attention to me instead of them. Other studies have found shelter dogs are more receptive to a female, and dogs meeting while walking on leash are more likely to fight if the walkers are male. Dogs taken care of by females tend to prefer women, and dogs primarily raised by men prefer men.

Bella, my first Newfoundland, was a big female and, like most Newfy puppies, friendly and inquisitive. She had an impressive pedigree and a calm, sweet personality. When I took her to puppy obedience classes, a heavy load rested on her furry shoulders. Like the first college student in a family, there were expectations beyond the previous generations after a slew of poorly trained Dolan dogs. Our training sessions included plentiful string cheese. However, the Canine Good Citizen final test is done without treats, like a trapeze performance without nets. Before the test, our dogs roughhoused like kids at an assembly. Bella tussled with Eva, her small Cocker Spaniel friend. The instructor, a former assistant principal at a Bronx High School, had a highly honed ability to overlook situations when his charges did not live up to expectations. Following a No Dog Left Behind educational principle, the young dogs all passed.

Breeders often recommend Ian Dunbar and Patricia McConnell as well-regarded trainers. A few training basics from Patricia McConnell's books include the following tips:

- Fear in puppies can grow into aggression in adult dogs, so to socialize your dog, find ways to create positive experiences with new people, places, and dogs.

- Find safe places to stimulate your pup, but do not overwhelm him while training. Initially, use places where there are few distractions.

- Remember, positive reinforcement is defined by your dog: whatever will encourage him to repeat the desired behavior. With Newfoundlands, this reward is likely to be treats, but it could also be praise or play with a favorite toy.

Photo Courtesy of Katie Dolan

Fun and Frequency

Your puppy will respond best to frequent, fun training sessions inter-spersed with your regular routines. Bring treats when you take your Newf for a walk, then practice Sit and Halt. Work on a long stay while you are watching television. Purchase a Squishy Face Studio flirt pole dog exercise toy and incorporate joyous play into your training of "leave it." Keep the end of the pole near the ground, as you do not want your growing Newf jumping up.

If you have another dog in your home, give both a cue and reward the duo when they do as you ask. I often work this way with Willow and Blue, who is old and somewhat arthritic. I ask Willow to sit while Blue simply stands next to her. I walk away and then release them to scamper toward me. They seem to love the competition.

Harnesses and Collars

Slip leashes and collars are often used in training yet can cause tracheal damage if improperly fitted. Straining at a collar placed too low on the dog's neck has been associated with thyroid disease, eye problems, back injuries, and tracheal damage. When training, the collar, whichever kind, should rest right behind the dog's ears, not low on the neck. It should be snug but allow room for two fingers to be placed between the dog and collar. For every day, some owners prefer martingales, which hang loosely but contract when necessary if attached to a leash.

Controlling the head controls the body, much like a halter on a 1,200-pound horse. Newfoundlands have been bred to pull heavy loads. A well-fitting harness should be used primarily for draft and hauling. A gentle halter or ThunderLeash (that wraps around your dog and hooks on the col-lar) will give you more control over a strong young Newf when walking or training.ainer

Finding a Trainer

Based on her research findings, Beth Strickler offers sage advice (See Box) on selecting a good instructor for training.

I had an embarrassing experience stemming from ineffectively training Bella. Karen Pryor, the dog trainer famous for clicker training, is a member of my animal behavior book group and came to my home one afternoon. My Bella was her usual self: following us around and fascinated by what we drank and ate as we sat by the fireplace on a cold wintery day. Bella made her move, and petite Karen had to wrestle her mug away from my dog. Karen gamely drank the remainder of her tea with a viscous coating of Newfoundland drool. I was mortified and knew it was my own fault. With Willow, I started training earlier and more diligently in the hope that she will eventually become both a therapy and a water rescue dog. As I've attended lessons with her over the past few months, I've realized the training is really for me. If I do things in the right sequence and with the right gestures and consistent words, Willow is a willing, proficient learner. Of course, treats help!

Photo Courtesy of Gary Baldwin

> **❝**
>
> *Because Newf pups grow so quickly, it is easy to forget that they are still babies and, like other puppies, have butterfly/hummingbird-sized brains. A big-dog body with a bird-sized brain.*
>
> **KATHY KOSIEROWSKI**
> *Dog Trainer*
>
> **❞**

Kathy Kosierowski, a dog trainer in Colorado, allowed me to summarize her training factsheets here, including general principles and specific cues. General principles for effective training include positive reinforcement, consistency, and capturing desirable behaviors by saying "Yes" or "Nice." Have your puppy work for what she wants, whether that's dinner, getting in the car, or playing with you. One person should assume overall responsibility for training your Newf, but all family members should learn the cues and apply them consistently.

> **❝**
>
> *I taught basic dog manners for many years at the local high school. We welcomed dogs of all ages. The first class always focused on "Attention," using the dog's name in a happy, upbeat voice with a kind facial expression. In fact, I had folks look in a mirror so they could see what their dog did while people were issuing commands. One example that proved quite effective was picturing an elementary school student staring out the window when the teacher was requesting a particular task. If they aren't looking at you, forget it!*
>
> *"Watch" is a most important first step. Proper usage of the dog's name is very important during initial training. I always say, "Your dog will let you know when you get it right!" There is no "one size fits all" way to train. Really depends on the personality of the dog. When people brought their school-age children to obedience class, the kids learned far more quickly than the adults!*
>
> **KAREN STEINROCK**
> *Newfoundland owner*
>
> **❞**

Find a quiet place without distractions to work on training with your dog. The pup should have already been exercised a bit, gone potty, and be ready

HOW TO SELECT A DOG TRAINER

Advice from Researcher Beth Strickler

1. Is the trainer using scientifically based training (potential key words to look for: reward-based training, force-free, and humane-training methods)?

2. Is the trainer a good teacher? Can the trainer communicate well with both humans and pets?

3. Is the trainer participating in continuing education?

4. Is the trainer requiring a relationship with a veterinarian (either for routine medical care, such as vaccines, and/or a medical evaluation for behavior problem)?

5. Is the trainer a member of or certified by a professional organization? (Note: certification does not ensure technique.)

6. Does the trainer have insurance?

7. Visit a class (evaluate cleanliness and trainer's interaction with clients and pets).

Walk away if

- Trainer uses choke collar, pinch collar, or electronic/shock collar.
- Trainer bans head collars of any kind.
- Trainer recommends physical reprimands of any kind (hitting, kicking, pinching, and so forth).
- Trainer uses word "alpha" or "dominant."

to pay attention to you. You will want to enroll in a puppy class to socialize your pup and get her used to the distractions of other dogs, and for you to practice the cues and consistent training. Here are some basics.

- **Sit:** With the pup standing, hold a treat at the nose. Slowly move the treat over the pup's head toward the rump. As soon as the pup's rump touches the ground, offer a happy "Yes" and give a treat. Add the hand gesture of holding up a finger to go along with a sit.

- **Down:** Hold the treat in hand and tell your pup to "sit" once. Put treat at pup's nose and move it slowly down toward the ground and away from her nose. Wait for the instant the pup's elbows touch the ground, say "Yes. Good down," and reward with treats on the ground between the pup's paws. Give a release cue of "go" or "okay" or whatever word you have selected.

- **Come/Touch:** Perhaps the most important thing to teach your growing dog is a reliable cue to come to you. Knowing and following this cue could save your dog's life. Decide what cue you are going to use and say it consistently. Many people say the dog's name first and then "Come." Adding clapping to your cue word works well. Research by Patricia McConnell found hand claps were more effective than words, whistles, or other sounds for getting a puppy to respond. Use your body language as well; turn slightly away from your dog and move away to encourage her to come along for the fun. You'll want to call her to you 20–30 times per day, in various parts of your house and outdoors in different settings. Be sure to call her when she is not so distracted that she will ignore you. The goal is to have her come reliably every time. Use the long line leash to work on "come" from a distance. It is okay to gently tug on the lead to get your pup heading toward you.

  Separate the dog's name from "Come" with a long pause. As she comes toward you, make noises, clap, or stomp your feet to encourage her, but do not repeat the cue. Praise when she comes to you and touches your target hand. Say "touch" as she does so and reward her with a treat. Never punish your dog when she comes to you, as you want her to associate coming with wonderful things. And never chase your puppy unless she is in immediate danger, and you must get her quickly.

- **Stay:** Ask for a "Sit" and then a "Stay." Gesture with a flat hand up signal for stay. When the pup has stayed for five seconds, give the release word "Go" or "Okay," and call her to you for a treat, praising. Repeat the exercise with longer stays.

- **Halt or Stop:** Another important skill to teach your growing dog is a reliable "Halt." When walking your dog on a loose leash, stop walking, cue "Stop," and pull back firmly on the leash. Reward your pup for stopping.

Repeat this cue frequently until your pup stops on her own when you cue her to do so.

> *One of my clients was walking with her dog, and they suddenly saw a mule deer in the field across the road. The dog went primal and started running toward the deer and road. A stop worked and probably saved the dog's life. You want to train your dog to stop and then wait for another cue from you. It might be come, or it might be stay, depending upon what is going on at the moment.*
>
> KATHY KOSIEROWSKI
> *Dog Trainer*

- **Eyes or Watch:** Ignoring distractions is a critical basic skill to teach your puppy. If she is not paying attention to you, she can't take your cues. This will allow you to walk your puppy in a busy park or down a crowded sidewalk or attend training classes together. You want to make yourself more exciting than anything else. Research on Golden Retrievers, German Shepherds, and Poodles suggests breed differences in holding a human's gaze. Newfoundlands, bred to work closely with humans, likely have a genetic predisposition to holding your gaze and take naturally to this cue (Jakovcevic et al. 2010).

  A simple way to build this skill is to teach "watch" or "eyes" to your puppy. Hold a treat or toy in front of her, bring the toy up between your eyes, praise (or click if you are clicker training), and give your dog the treat. After several repetitions, bring your hand to your face without a treat in it. When your dog looks at you, immediately say "yes" and give her a treat or start to play with a toy you have in your other hand or in a pocket. When your puppy begins following your hand as a physical cue to look at your face, you can add in a verbal cue of your choice, like "eyes" or "watch."

- **Leave It:** This cue is obviously important to prevent the ingestion of a dropped medication or other potentially dangerous objects and helps to keep a dog from lunging toward other dogs during walks, etc. When walking by an attractive object (like another dog or a candy wrapper on the ground) say a low, sharp "leave it" with a quick tug on the collar, then continue walking. Most dogs learn this cue in about 10 minutes. One trainer had people bring in things their dogs really liked (one lady brought a brassiere!) to practice "leave it" in class.

> *All good dog owners also play games with their dogs. These games are important. They help us to establish our relationships with our dogs and to learn to know our dogs better. When we play with our dogs, we and our dogs must communicate to cooperate. The dogs speak dog but understand English; we speak English and understand dog, and the communication works. Some games are standard, like chase and fetch. Often, though, the most rewarding games are those that we and our dogs make up new. I play "go find" with our girls, hiding small dog biscuits around the living room while the girls are on a down-stay out of sight in the kitchen.*
>
> **ROGER FREY,**
> *from Play with Your Dog (Roger, who died in 2021, was a beloved NCA Board member and breed expert who taught water rescue to many Newfs.)*

Correcting Unwanted Behaviors

You'll also want to be ready to correct unwanted behaviors. For large Newfs, it is especially important to eliminate jumping up on people. Judicious use of "NO" in a low and assertive voice is important.

Jumping Up: It's cute when they're little but can be quite daunting as they grow. It's best to correct it early. Since "Down" is used for other purposes, "OFF" is an effective cue for jumping up. Pesky demands for attention, such as nipping or barking in your face, are often best handled by simply ignoring the pup for about five minutes. Walk away, closing a door behind you if necessary. The worst punishment is removing your attention from your Newf altogether. This takes time and practice, but eventually, they figure out that behaving translates into your attention.

Nipping: Never hit your dog on the nose when she nips you. Instead, get up and walk away, forcing your pup to be alone for what to her will be an excruciating five minutes. Go back, try again, and if she continues nipping, repeat the process. Make sure she has plenty of quality chew objects available around the house, but don't offer one when she nips. This could be misconstrued as a reward.

Barking: Pay attention to barking communications and acknowledge by saying, "It's okay" if your dog is appropriately warning you about a new situation. Use the cue "Quiet" if your dog is excessively barking, remove her from the distraction and praise a "good quiet." She will eventually learn that good things happen when she stops barking. Incidentally, Josh barked joyously when he won Best in Show at the Westminster Dog Show.

Photo Courtesy of Heidi Peterson

Photo Courtesy of Katie Dolan

Cues for Working Dogs

With puppies likely to be shown in conformation or trained as water rescue dogs, it is helpful to prepare them for some specific behaviors in the chosen activity. For example, "take," "hold," and "give" are important skills to teach a future water dog as is "fetch" using a bumper. Judi Adler's The Newfoundland Puppy: Early Care, Early Training is a great resource for the best ways to teach additional cues. See the Notes and Resources chapter for information on ordering the book.

CHAPTER 7
Exercise

> "
>
> *Pups require rest periods between play sessions. Remember, pup-pies are babies; they cannot take the stress of accompanying a distance jogger. Be careful on ice and snow or waxed or otherwise slippery floors. Grass or gravel are the best surfaces for exercise.*
>
> BENITA EDDS
> *Timberknoll Newfoundlands*
>
> "

The Value of Exercise

The English have an expression: "For the first year, the puppy should play in the garden." This means a safely fenced yard, off-leash. Regular, regulated exercise works best for a Newf and is critical to keep your dog happy, trim, and engaged. Boredom and restlessness from a lack of exercise can lead to problem behaviors like chewing and digging. Going on a walk or a swim also keeps Newfoundlands mentally stimulated. They can be couch potatoes if you let them laze around the house all day.

Puppies

Jogging, slippery floors, and prolonged walking are the main causes of joint disorders in growing pups. A puppy should go on walks no longer than one minute for every week of its age.

Photo Courtesy of Katie Dolan

Young Dogs

Juvenile Newfs are full of energy and get the zoomies, where they run around exuberantly and jump off anything in the vicinity. Unfortunately, excessive exercise can cause harm because the joints used during exercise are where the dog's growth plates are located. The Newfoundland Health and Longevity Committee cautions, "If you have a young dog, you need to be his advocate because he doesn't have a sense of self-preservation. Your pup is growing at an exponential rate (four pounds per week), and even if he does not show any pain or discomfort, repeated high-impact activity can cause long-term joint issues." Continued minor muscle and growth plate strains can make your Newf vulnerable to future injuries, including sprains and ligament tears.

You may recall the NCA image of a Newf's growth plate closures from Chapter Five. Please refer back to it as a reference.

BASIC TIPS FOR INJURY PREVENTION:

- Dog parks and doggie daycare can be dangerous for young dogs because of the uncontrolled exercise with lots of high-impact movements during play with dogs of various sizes. In addition, the risk of injury (dog attacks and biting) is high.

- For fetch play: Roll the ball to ensure it doesn't take a bad hop and encourage a dangerous jump.

- For a flirt pole: Drag it on the ground, encouraging your young dog to chase it without jumping vertically.

- For tug play: Stay low! Control the fun by keeping your dog's four paws on the ground while you tug.

- Create safe interactions by limiting play sessions to one-on-one with similar size and age playmates.

> **"**
>
> *Newfs should never exercise on hard surfaces like asphalt and cement. Walks are best on unpaved surfaces. Although Newfs can jump into and out of trucks and cars, such activities place tremendous stress on ligaments and joints. Training Newfs to enter and exit the vehicle on a ramp will help preserve ligaments and joints for their lifetime. Where a ramp isn't available, the human should assist by physically supporting the dog's entry and exit.*
>
> DR. JUDITH ZIFFER,
> *Sandy Cove Newfoundlands*
>
> **"**

Adult Dogs

Do not take your puppy jogging until she is at least two years old and the growth plates on her shoulders, elbows, and hips are fully closed. As with human "weekend warriors," exercising only a day or two per week can lead to injury. A consistent level of daily exercise is best. "On the one hand, we know wolves run with their packs for miles. On the other, we know that the risks for a sedentary puppy with a weekend-warrior exercise pattern are worse than for a puppy that gets continuous, self-regulated exercise," says Dr. Marc Wosar, an orthopedic specialist quoted on the AKC website. "Unfortunately, there are no hard-and-fast rules. Your veterinarian is a great

*Photo Courtesy
of Sabrina Conci*

place to start your research." You can also speak with your breeder, contact breed enthusiast groups for advice, and talk to other owners about their experience with Newfs. Watch your dog carefully for signs of excessive tiredness or lameness, as this could be a symptom of too much exercise or a more serious problem.

When your Newf is full-sized, dog parks are one option for exercise and playtime with other dogs. Parks with separate areas for big and small dogs are the preferred setup. If dogs of all sizes frequent your local dog park, you can teach your dog a "down/stay" when a smaller dog approaches so the smaller dog is not frightened. Bear in mind that things can quickly escalate in a dog park: unpredictable dog dynamics, the presence of children, and resource guarding over treats may lead to unhappy outcomes.

Swimming

Swimming is the best form of exercise for your Newf. Introduce your puppy to the water in an outdoor plastic pool and to a real body of water at four months of age. Preferably, the lake, pond, or ocean should have a gradually sloping beach. Many beaches are open to dogs during the wintertime and after-hours.

*Photo Courtesy
of Katie Dolan*

Walks

Daily walks with your Newf should be a fun experience for both of you if your dog has been trained to walk on a leash and not pull you around the neighborhood.

We live high in the mountains of Colorado, and our dogs love a walk in the woods or along the street past the interesting smells of other dogs and houses. Because a full-grown Newf looks a lot like a black bear, I put orange vests on my dogs—even outside of hunting season—so hikers do not get frightened by an erroneous bear sighting on the trail.

Play Sessions

Some play suggestions for you and your Newf:

- For "fetch/play" with a Newfoundland, ensure the ball you are using is substantial enough not to be swallowed. Kong makes a medium-sized retrieve ball that squeaks and is nicely soft to the dog's grip. Tennis balls are typically too small to be safe for the breed at maturity. Water bumpers are great retrieve objects, as most Newfs are immediately drawn to the texture.

- During foul weather days when you're stuck inside, play indoor games such as "find it," hiding toys around the house.
- Another fun exercise is using small traffic cones to practice heeling, turns, halts, figure eights, you name it.
- Purchase a flirt pole and play with your pup.
- A mentally "exercised" Newf gets just as played out as one that took a two-mile walk!
- Use puzzle games, Kongs, and snuffle mats with hidden food.
- Put treats or dog food into things such as paper towel rolls or plastic bottles to make your own puzzles.

PLAYING IN PUBLIC PLACES

One study found dogs on a leash sniffed one another significantly less often than dogs off-leash, and (no surprise!) males sniffed females more often. Small dogs sniffed larger dogs less often than individuals of the same size (Petr Rezáč et al., 2011).

Another study found smaller dogs are less likely to approach a life-size dog replica of a Labrador Retriever than larger dogs (Leaver & Reimchen, 2008).

Playing is a frequent behavior when one dog encounters another dog in a public place; however, play occurred less frequently when both dogs were leashed versus both dogs off a leash. Play was observed in two-thirds of the puppies; senior dogs were eleven times less likely to play than puppies (Petr Rezáč et al., 2011).

- Make "pupsicles" with low-sodium chicken or bone broth. Add kibble, peanut butter (non-xylitol), yogurt, blueberries, or canned dog food, and freeze.

- Scent and Search games: Hide dog food or a favorite toy around the house and use a cue such as "search." A variation is to hide the rewards under a pile of blankets in your living room. (Sounds a bit messy to me!)

- Create a small sandpit in your backyard and let your Newf dig for treasures.

- Make your backyard area an interesting play area with tunnels, logs, agility toys, traffic cones, etc.

Photo Courtesy
of Sabrina Conci

*Photo Courtesy
of Heidi Peterson*

Mental Stimulation

Research suggests owners of large breeds such as Newfoundlands spend more time playing with their dogs than owners of smaller breeds. Play, whether fetch or using a flirt pole or hiding treats, is a great way to bond with your pup and one of the best ways to keep her stimulated. Of course, working towards an obedience, water rescue, rally, or other title (See Working Newfs chapter) is another fun way to keep your dog mentally challenged and alert.

CHAPTER 8
Socializing Your Newfoundland

> **"**
>
> **I am the noble Newfoundland,**
> **My voice is loud and deep**
> **I keep watch all through the night,**
> **While other people sleep.**
> *(Children's song popular in the 1880s)*
>
> **"**

Despite the night watchman attributes of the breed expressed in this children's song, our two Newfs sleep more soundly and deeply than the humans in our household, often snoring loudly! The song, however, does suggest the attentiveness and noble aspects of a Newf. Having a Newfy who is well-adjusted and confident is critical, especially given the breed's size and strength.

Importance of Socialization

The watchwords for socializing are early, eclectic, and every day, in different settings, with people of all ages, and with new dogs and other animals. Start taking your dog out to public places once your veterinarian says it is safe, and she'll learn to behave in a variety of situations and enjoy interacting with different people. Many behavioral problems in adult dogs, including separation anxiety, reactivity, and fear of strangers, stem from inadequate puppy socialization. On the other side of the coin, more socialization and experiences translate into a quick ability to learn and more inquisitiveness.

According to the American Association of Veterinary Behaviorists, "Behavioral issues, not infectious diseases, are the number one cause of

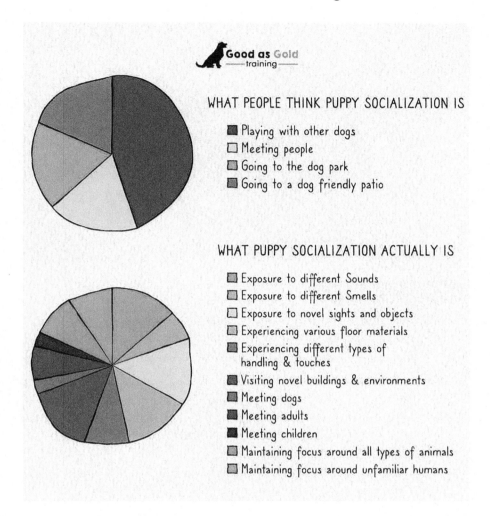

Good as Gold
——— training ———

WHAT PEOPLE THINK PUPPY SOCIALIZATION IS

■ Playing with other dogs
□ Meeting people
◩ Going to the dog park
■ Going to a dog friendly patio

WHAT PUPPY SOCIALIZATION ACTUALLY IS

◩ Exposure to different Sounds
◩ Exposure to different Smells
□ Exposure to novel sights and objects
◩ Experiencing various floor materials
■ Experiencing different types of handling & touches
■ Visiting novel buildings & environments
■ Meeting dogs
■ Meeting adults
■ Meeting children
◩ Maintaining focus around all types of animals
◩ Maintaining focus around unfamiliar humans

death for dogs under three years of age" and are the primary reason why dogs are surrendered to shelters. The clear benefits of early socialization offset the low risk of infection for a puppy in the process of getting vaccinated. Despite growing evidence about the importance of socialization, Cutler (2017) found nearly one-third of pups in the U.S. are insufficiently exposed to other dogs and humans. Studies also show pups raised by owners who get expert advice on dog behavior are less likely to have problems.

Although your Newf has been bred for her sweet disposition and temperament, you'll want to give her many chances to experience new people, places, and pets. Here are a few suggestions:

Photo Courtesy of Heidi Peterson

Puppy Parties

For early puppy parties, invite several mild-mannered, Newf-friendly humans who don't mind drool to play with your puppy.

- Let the mild-mannered humans feed treats to your pup.
- Then gradually add small children, loud adults, and other groups into your home.
- Adult dogs visiting the pup should have all vaccinations and should be chosen with caution. A puppy party should initially last no more than thirty minutes.
- Gradually, bring your puppy to other homes, quiet parks, and, finally, busy public places.

> **"**
>
> *Dog socialization should start young, but do not overdo. Also, be very careful around unknown dogs. I do not let anyone come up to me with a dog and let them play. Scheduled puppy playtime with friends' puppies is best. Also, the size of the puppy for playing is crucial. It must be roughly the same size as the Newf puppy, so no one gets hurt. Places like Home Depot are also great adventures for puppies.*
>
> AMY CULVER DAVIS
> *Birchbark Newfoundlands*
>
> **"**

Socialization with People

Dogs and people have evolved to benefit greatly from each other's company. Here are a few highlights on the intense, wonderful bonds between humans and their dogs:

- Nearly all owners talk to their dogs; 81% view the dog as a family member.
- A "shockingly high" number of people claim they would save their pets before they would save a fellow human being in certain life-threatening situations.
- Attachment to pets is highest among people living alone and couples who do not have children living at home.
- A dog is more likely to reduce stress than a spouse.
- "In the Family Life Space Diagram, people are asked to pictorially represent their significant relationships. More than a third place themselves closer to their dog than to another family member". (Barker & Barker, 1988) *I love the researchers' names—they were clearly destined to be canine researchers!*
- When a human and dog play, both have higher levels of oxytocin and dopamine in their blood serum. In the human, stress hormones are lowered.

Photo Courtesy of Katie Dolan

Photo Courtesy of The Zimmerman Collection

As Jennifer Vanpola of WhiteHouse Farm notes, "Walking a Newf can be like being out with a Kardashian. You are swamped. People take photos and ask, 'How much does he weigh?' and take photos." Indeed, when I walk our Newfoundlands, people seek us out to say hello and tell me about the Newfoundland they knew growing up. Some ask before petting my dogs, but many assume a Newfoundland is just going to be friendly. Fortunately, my dogs love every human they meet!

Socialization with Children

Newfoundlands, the nanny dogs, generally take to children immediately and are always listed as one of the top breeds for families. As we've already seen, loud, energetic, quick-moving, unpredictable children can make a dog nervous. That said, the management challenges are twofold: teaching children how to be good citizens with canines and teaching your large Newf to be calm and not jump up on children. Your Newf should know her basic obedience cues and be ready to immediately commence a sit/stay where needed. Toddlers and small children should be reminded not to:

- Pull tails
- Yank on ears
- Try to ride horseback on the Newf
- Run away from the dog squealing

Older children should also be reminded not to leave electronics, clothes, eyeglasses, socks, or anything else where the dog might find these items.

With all those caveats, don't forget that your sweet nanny dog is likely to love playing with kids. Some canine-child games you can organize for fun include:

- Fetch and ball toss
- Hide and seek
- Basic obedience cues with rewards (remind kids to give a treat with an open palm at the dog's level so she doesn't jump up to get the treat)
- Find the object
- Dig in sand
- Splash in a lake or backyard puppy pool
- Flirt pole games

Photo Courtesy of Cissy Sullivan

Socialization with Other Dogs in Household

When introducing a puppy to a senior dog in the house, be aware that senior dogs have an established routine and may not like puppy disruptions. The dogs should be introduced to one another on neutral ground (as noted in the Homecoming chapter). Make sure your senior dog is given time away from the puppy. American Kennel Club veterinarian Dr. Jerry Klein notes, "Small gestures can make a huge difference in the attitude of your older dog" and suggests:

- Focus attention on your older dog before greeting your younger dog.
- Feed the older dog first.
- Put the leash on your older dog first.

After your first Newfoundland has matured, you might want to join the many Newf owners who add a second or third Newf to their family. According to the Newfoundland Club of America data from 2017, nearly 30% of their members own two dogs.

Photo Courtesy of Katie Dolan

Socialization at Dog Parks

Newfoundland breeders generally believe dog parks are not a good place to socialize young pups. You do not know the other dogs or their health and vaccination status. You do not want the early experiences of your puppy with other dogs to be negative. Once your dog is older, dog parks can be fun places to go. Visit without your dog at various times of the day to assess who are the regular attendees and gauge if your dog will feel comfortable and safe. The other dogs and their owners can be unpredictable, so pause at the entranceway and check out the vibes. Additionally, you can have your dog sniff and greet other dogs through the fence so that you can gauge friendliness. Some parks have separate areas for big dogs and little dogs, which makes playing easier.

It is extremely important for young dogs to experience happy, friendly interactions with other dogs.

SHEILA MALLINSON
Kodiak Acres Newfoundlands

As an alternative to dog parks, some dog trainers offer safe drop-in times where dogs that have taken courses at the obedience school can stop by for more socialization with other dogs they've met in class.

Socializing with Other Animals

As described in a previous chapter, be sure to introduce your Newf to any cats in the household in a supervised way, with the dog on a leash. You might also want to put the new arrival in his crate and let the cat approach and sniff the dog. The same basic approach would be used with livestock on a farm; keep the dog leashed and closely supervise the interactions until the animals become comfortable with one another.

SOCIALIZATION STUDIES

Critical Socialization Period: The critical socialization period appears to vary by breed and canid species. Kathryn Lord compared three litters of wolves and seven litters of Border Collies and German Shepherds to test early responses to olfactory, auditory, and visual stimuli. Wolves and dogs both develop olfaction by two weeks, hearing by four weeks, and vision by six weeks on average. However, wolves begin exploring their environment and are mobile at two weeks, when they must rely only on a sense of smell because their other senses are not yet developed. Wolves cue on scent, which varies from human to human, so human-reared wolves never generalize to feel comfortable with other humans besides the ones that rear them.

For puppies, the critical socialization period begins at four weeks (when a puppy will readily explore) and ends at eight weeks, when a pup will only reluctantly approach a novel object. Therefore, dogs have four weeks to interact with their environment with adult senses and little fear. Lord looked at why German Shepherds fail as service dogs, mostly due to fear of new situations. At a five-week veterinary exam, Labrador Retriever puppies showed little fear and happily wagged their tails, while most of the German Shepherd puppies were already fearful. These results suggest fear of novelty develops at an earlier age among German Shepherds. Also, female Shepherd pups tend to be smaller. Having been terrorized by her bigger siblings in the kennel situation, the smallest female of a litter frequently failed service school.

During this period, it's important to expose a pup to any stimulation she might confront in her adult life. This can even be done virtually! Pluijmakers et al. (2010) show exposure of pups at three to five weeks of age to various images on video reduces their fear responses at eight weeks. Primary social relationship in dogs is formed with littermates through play fighting and promotes the formation of the pack. As discussed in the Finding Your Newf chapter, research shows an increased incidence of behavioral disorders (fear and aggression toward other dogs and humans) in dogs bred by commercial breeders, puppy farms, and pet stores due in part to inadequate socialization.

Late Socialization Period (12 weeks to 6 months): Juvenile dogs require continued socialization. A study of guide dogs found the rehomed puppies were more likely to succeed as guide dogs than pups who remained in the kennel. In addition, juvenile dogs exposed to busy urban environments are less likely to show aggression toward unfamiliar people later in life.

CHAPTER 9
Nutrition

> "
>
> *A man is not a good man to me because he will feed me if I should be starving, or warm me if I should be freezing, or pull me out of a ditch if I should ever fall into one. I can find you a Newfoundland dog that will do as much.*
>
> HENRY DAVID THOREAU
> *Walden*
>
> "

Learn the lingo. Do your research using trusted, fact-based websites. Account for treat calories. Adjust for the dog's age. Myths abound. These are the key phrases relevant to your dog's nutrition.

Why Is Nutrition so Important

If there is one area where a new puppy owner is likely to receive confusing and conflicting advice, it is about a dog's nutrition. Although there is strong veterinary nutrition science about canine dietary requirements, life-stage nutrition, and more, myths persist surrounding raw food, grain-free dog foods, and the use of supplements. Unlike wolves, who are likely to get their food through hunting and consuming prey, dogs have evolved to also be adept scavengers and to eat and metabolize a wide variety of foods. This variety translates into sometimes confusing choices for pet owners. Because they develop slowly and have a lower metabolic rate than other breeds, Newfoundlands have unique nutritional needs and concerns. This chapter includes suggestions from longtime Newfoundland breeders as well as the most recent science from the nation's veterinary schools and pet food manufacturers.

Any diet should be appropriate to the dog's age (puppy, adult, or senior). Some dogs are prone to becoming overweight, so watch your dog's calorie consumption and body condition score. Treats can be an important aid in training, but giving too many can cause obesity or unbalance your dog's diet. (Veterinarian nutritionists recommend that treats should be no more than 10% of a dog's daily calories.) Research which human foods are safe for dogs and which are not. Check with your veterinarian if you have any concerns about your dog's weight or diet. Avoid feeding a growing Newfoundland pup a home-cooked diet unless you are working closely with a veterinary nutritionist, as mistakes can be dangerous and cause permanent damage. If you wish to feed your adult Newf a home-cooked diet, be sure again to work with a board-certified veterinary nutritionist so that the recipe you use meets the dog's unique nutritional needs.

Feeding Puppies

If you are bringing home a puppy, it is best to give him the same diet he has been eating with its littermates for the first week or two. This will minimize digestive disruption as he copes with many new things in his new home. Puppies metabolize excess calcium differently than adults, which is one of the reasons why large and giant-breed puppies should eat a large-breed puppy food that "meets the requirements for growth, including growth of

Photo Courtesy of Katie Dolan

large-size dogs" or that has gone through feeding trials for growth. Newf puppies should not be overfed, should not gain more than four pounds per week, and should stay trim (at a four or five on the nine-point body condition scale) throughout growth. Being able to count the ribs on your pup through his fur is an easy way to gauge that his weight is just right.

This is the other advantage of large-breed puppy foods—they tend to be lower in calories per cup than regular puppy foods but are more concentrated in all the essential nutrients like protein, vitamins, and minerals. They help your pup grow slowly without the risk of nutritional deficiencies.

Weigh your pup every three to four weeks to make sure she is not gaining weight too fast. Vary the types of bowls and feeding locations to prevent your dog from focusing on food being served in only one way. Veterinary nutritionists generally recommend feeding large-breed puppies a large-breed puppy food up until 18 months of age to help them grow at an optimal rate, provide the right amount of calcium, and minimize the risk for deficiencies of nutrients.

As Your Dog Grows

When your dog is spayed or neutered, its caloric requirements are reduced by up to 30%, so be sure to reduce the amount of food after sterilization. In addition, an older dog who may be more sedentary does not require as many calories as a young dog.

General Feeding Tips and Considerations:

- Use steel bowls and clean the bowls daily with dish soap and water.
- Consider using food-dispensing toys, as they have been found to increase activity levels and may help keep your Newf trim.
- Many breeders follow the "puppy rule of 12" about the importance of a dozen different experiences, be it food containers or locations to be fed, surfaces to walk upon, loud noises, and unexpected objects. Dogs accustomed to more experiences will take new experiences in stride.
- If possible, keep the dog food and feeding away from your kitchen so that the Newf does not associate her food with your food.
- Breeders and veterinarians often recommend changing kibble brands every so often. On the other hand, some experts believe, "If it isn't broke,

don't fix it." Some brands are formulated with different flavors to provide taste variety without digestive problems.

- While kibble may modestly aid in reducing tartar on some of your dog's smaller teeth, you should still brush his teeth daily to promote optimal dental health.

- Be aware of any recalls, as they can happen with even the best dog food companies.

Dog Food Choices

The WSAVA (World Small Animal Veterinary Association) developed criteria by which the quality and nutritional quality of a pet food can be judged. Questions you should ask include: Do they employ a full-time qualified nutritionist? What are the quality control procedures for ingredients and finished products? Has the manufacturer undertaken research or had nutritional studies published in peer-reviewed journals? The Pet Nutrition Alliance's Dare to Ask tool provides answers to some of these questions, which can help in deciding what dog food to select:

https://petnutritionalliance.org/site/pnatool/dare-to-ask-we-did/

Grain-free Dog Foods

In 2017, veterinarians began seeing an increase in the number of dogs with severe canine heart disease (DCM or dilated cardiomyopathy). The Food and Drug Administration soon issued an alert about a possible link with certain dog foods, which were often grain-free and commonly contained peas and lentils. Canine DCM, a severe disease of the heart muscle, is the second most common heart disease affecting pet dogs, with a prevalence over 50 percent in breeds such as the Doberman Pinscher. DCM causes the heart to grow bigger and its contractions weaker. Ultimately, the disease can end in heart failure and death. Large-dog breeds (including Newfoundlands) are genetically susceptible to DCM. However, research suggests certain ingredients in dog food, such as peas, may be associated with diet-associated DCM. Stay up to date on this rapidly evolving situation. It is also important to know that there are no health benefits to grain-free diets.

Raw and Human Grade Dog Food

Some breeders swear by the virtues of meat-based raw dog foods, but there is no scientific evidence of any health benefits. In addition, many studies suggest raw foods are commonly contaminated with bacterial pathogens, thereby increasing the risk of illness for both dogs and humans handling the food. Raw dog foods have been linked to neurological issues, obstructions due to choking on bones, and hyperthyroidism. In addition, some therapy animal programs will not allow participation by dogs being fed meat-based raw food due to the possibility of spreading pathogens to immune-compromised patients in health care settings. Raw meat–based diets are discouraged because of their high risks and lack of health benefits.

Freeze dried raw is the safest alternative if you decide to feed a raw diet. You'll also read about and may want to consider feeding Human Grade dog foods, which use ingredients that would meet human consumption standards. Contrary to some popular belief, many human foods (cut carrots, chicken, beef, green beans, yogurt, cottage cheese, bananas, eggs, etc.) in moderation can be very healthy supplements in your dog's diet. (See Resource chapter for timely articles about these options.)

Dietary Supplements

Some breeders recommend Vitamin C and other vitamin supplements; however, a high-quality commercial diet contains all the vitamins and minerals a dog needs. In fact, toxicity can be a problem with some supplements. In addition, vitamins and other dietary supplements are not regulated by the FDA in the same way as drugs, so the quality and quantity in these supplements vary widely. Dietary supplements may have benefits for certain health conditions, but it's always important to work with your veterinarian or a veterinary nutritionist to decide on appropriate supplements, doses, and specific brands that have independent testing of quality control. Many breeders recommend glucosamine and other supplements to help prevent joint issues later in life.

The Overweight Newfoundland

Being overweight or obese is associated with multiple health conditions and is especially a problem for Newfoundlands, as it puts them at high risk for orthopedic injuries. Being heavy can also aggravate heart problems and cause diabetes. The Golden Retriever Lifetime survey (see details in Health chapter) found that overweight or obese spayed/neutered dogs have a 300% greater chance of orthopedic injuries, but keeping them trim throughout their lives can significantly reduce the risk.

Most dog owners believe their overweight dogs are close to perfect, so efforts are underway to educate pet owners on how to assess their dogs' body condition and muscle tone. In addition, the Pet Nutrition Alliance (pet-nutritionalliance.org) offers a calorie calculator for dogs to give a starting point for the number of calories your dog needs. But every dog is an individual, and Newfs tend to have low metabolic rates, so it's important to use the body condition score chart to be sure your dog stays at a four or five on the nine-point body condition scale throughout her life. (See Resources chapter for details.)

CHAPTER 10
Health

Heredity, veterinary care, testing, vaccinations, common ailments, spay/neutering, and basic first aid are the watchwords for your Newfoundland's health. All these aspects of veterinary care combine with training, nutrition, exercise, and socialization to influence the health, longevity, and quality of life for a Newf. Because heredity plays a role in many Newfoundland health problems, it is

C.H.I.C.

Hips evaluated by OFA at 24 months for dysplasia

Heart cleared by a cardiologist at 12 months

DNA or parentage tested for cystinuria

Elbows evaluated by OFA at 24 months for dysplasia

FOUNDATION OF A HEALTHY NEWFOUNDLAND

important to obtain a dog from a reputable breeder. Newfs are at risk for a range of problems, but healthy lineages dramatically reduce the chance of illness. This chapter describes the ailments that might affect your Newfoundland and provides information about health certifications, pet insurance, when to spay and neuter, first aid resources, and common canine accidents.

Health Certifications

As you may recall from the chapter on finding your new Newfoundland, health certifications are a critical component of the process. OFA has an online database (Canine Health Information Center) for canine genetics research. A reputable Newfoundland breeder will have completed a cardiology clearance by a board-certified veterinary cardiologist when the puppies are 10 weeks old. As the graphic from the Newfoundland Health Foundation illustrates, the following tests are recommended by age two for Newfs who are going to be bred:

- X-rays for hip dysplasia, elbow, and patella
- Echocardiogram and cardiac exam by a board-certified veterinary cardiologist
- Eye exam performed by a board-certified veterinary ophthalmologist
- Cystinuria clearance (if both parents are clear, this is not an issue)
- Thyroid testing, if warranted

> **"**
>
> *A Newf's health begins generations before the pup is conceived. The gene pool sets in motion the hereditary characteristics for the dog. Anyone considering a Newf should go to the website for OFA for information regarding health clearances of the pup's ancestors. The known history of heart problems, elbow issues, hip issues, eye conditions, thyroid disorders, and cystinuria are listed on OFA. The more clearances that ancestors have posted, the greater the likelihood that the puppy about to join the family will also receive these health clearances as an adult. The importance of ancestral clearances and illnesses can't be overstated.*
>
> **DR. JUDITH M. ZIFFER**
> *Sandy Cove Newfoundlands*
>
> **"**

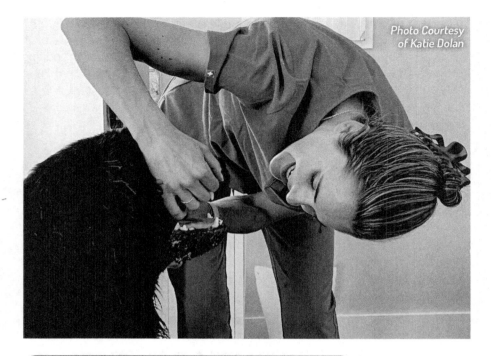

Photo Courtesy of Katie Dolan

Common Newfoundland Ailments

One Newfoundland guide lists 28 different health problems for the breed; the list is perhaps overly dramatic, especially if you have researched the health lineages for your dog. The breed is susceptible to eye maladies, glandular diseases, blood diseases, and cystinuria (which causes kidney issues and can be ruled out by genetic testing), but the major areas of health concern are as follows:

Heart: Sub-valvular aortic stenosis (SAS) and pulmonic stenosis are congenital narrowings of specific heart valves. The SAS incidence rate in Newfoundlands is 4 percent, roughly 10 times higher than in the general population of dogs. In addition, several other heart conditions can be diagnosed in puppies and treated. That is why it is so important that your Newf puppy be examined by a board-certified cardiologist-veterinarian. A murmur in a Newfoundland is considered SAS until an echocardiogram proves otherwise. Genetic cardiomyopathy causes weakness in the muscle tissues of the heart, which can lead to enlargement of the heart and heart failure. DCM can also possibly develop due to feeding certain dog foods (see Nutrition chapter).

Orthopedic Issues: Hip dysplasia can occur in all dog breeds but is particularly prevalent in large and giant dogs. According to the OFA database, hip dysplasia affects 26% of Newfs, while elbow dysplasia affects 23%. There is a genetic component to these orthopedic problems as several genes interact, so hips and elbows are certified in the OFA database, and reputable breeders test their dogs for these conditions before breeding them. In addition, Newfoundlands are susceptible to cruciate and cranial ligament tears as well as luxating patella (a slipping kneecap). The chance of an orthopedic injury can be reduced by careful monitoring of a pup's growth rate and attention to the dog's weight. The pain associated with these orthopedic issues can be managed by a range of medications, physical therapy, and, in cases of severe dysplasia or in young dogs, surgery.

Bloat/Gastric Dilatation Volvulus (GDV): In this life-threatening condition, gas is created as fermentation occurs in the stomach, the dog's stomach rotates on its long axis, and the blood supply is cut off. There are many myths about preventive measures for GDV, but these have not been confirmed by the research. Heredity, advancing age, anatomy, and whether the dog is anxious are confirmed bloat-risk factors. These studies suggest it may be risky to board a nervous Newf. Common sense and the wisdom of longtime breeders suggest that intense exercising before or after eating meals should be avoided. Breeds with deep chests and longer ligaments are

BLOAT

Anxious, Restless, Pacing

Excessive Drooling

Attempts to Vomit (white foam)

Distended/Hard Abdomen

more susceptible to bloat; males are more likely to develop bloat as they reach the prime of life.

A gastropexy, which surgically staples the dog's stomach so it cannot flip, is highly effective and can be done either as a stand-alone procedure or at the time of spay/neutering. Indeed, consideration is being given to providing routine gastropexy for all high-risk breeds at spay/neuter clinics.

> **❝**
>
> *In the nearly 70 years that I've had Newfoundlands, I have never had a dog torse that was tacked. Sadly, in September 2021, because of the pandemic, I put off a gastropexy for a three-year-old Newf. He torsed and died. Jessy's death would have been prevented had I done what I knew needed to be done. It is saddest to have a Newfy die from something that could have and should have been prevented.*
>
> DR. JUDITH M. ZIFFER
> *Sandy Cove Newfoundlands*
> ***"Torsed" refers to the twisting of the stomach that accompanies bloat; "tacked" refers to a gastropexy procedure.**
>
> **❞**

Eyes: An increasing focus (no pun intended) on Newf eyes is occurring. At a recent health clearance clinic for over 60 Newfs likely to be bred, 25% did not have clear eyes, mostly because of cataracts. Experts now recommend that eyes be checked on an annual basis, according to Lou Ann Lenner, a member of the NCA Health and Longevity Committee.

Cancers: Newfs are susceptible to several kinds of cancer, including testicular cancer and osteosarcoma, which is a malignant form of bone cancer (usually in the bones of the shoulder and knee) that causes rapid onset of lameness and requires aggressive treatment.

Forelimb Anomaly (Congenital Radial Head Luxation): Forelimb anomaly is an often-debilitating deformity of the elbow joint that is most likely genetic. It has been officially diagnosed in Newfoundlands, Bernese Mountain Dogs, Tibetan Mastiffs, and Akitas. Currently, a DNA study is underway through the Morris Animal Foundation with funding provided by the Newfoundland Club of America Charitable Trust, and it is hoped that a genetic test for the disease will be developed.

Heatstroke: Do not walk your Newf in hot temperatures or put her in a hot car. Keep her cool with fans where possible. Like all dogs, Newfs sweat through glands in their mouth and on their paws. Spray your pup's paws with tepid water. If dogs get too hot, they can go into shock, so keep an eye on your Newf's behavior and check her pulse. The resting heartbeat should be 60–100 beats per minute for adults and over 120 beats for puppies. If your dog is very lethargic or has a fast heart rate, seek veterinary care.

When to Spay or Neuter

The answers to this question for Newfoundlands and other breeds are complicated and have evolved as new research findings emerge. It is an area where people of goodwill often disagree. A growing number of experts conclude Newfoundlands should not be sterilized until after their long bones are fully grown, and the rubbery joints become solid at two years of age, while others recommend waiting until three years of age.

The Morris Animal Foundation Golden Retriever Lifetime Study gathers ongoing information on 3,000 Golden Retrievers from around the United States to identify the nutritional, environmental, lifestyle, and genetic risk

ANATOMY OF A DOG

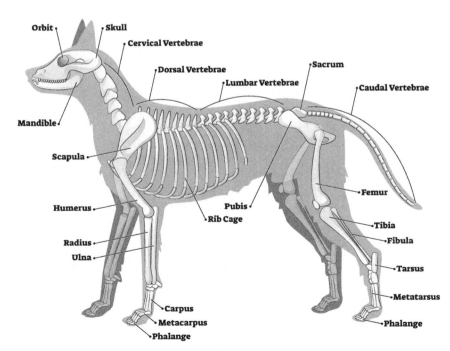

factors for cancer and other diseases in dogs. Owners and veterinarians complete yearly questionnaires about the health status and lifestyles of the dogs. Biological samples are collected, and each dog has a physical examination annually. The study suggests spay/neutering is a risk factor, especially in large breeds, for weight issues. A dog spayed or neutered at one year of age is twice as likely to become overweight or obese. In addition, the youngest dogs, which had not gone through any sort of pubertal changes when spayed/neutered, had the highest risk for orthopedic injuries. Spayed/neutered dogs that were overweight or obese had a 300% greater chance of orthopedic injuries.

It should also be noted that sterilization of dogs is not permitted in Norway. Spay/neutering will not make a dog less aggressive or less likely to wander and some research suggests dogs neutered or spayed between 7 and 12 months of age are more likely to demonstrate aggression towards strangers (Farhoody et al., 2018).

On the other hand, spay/neutering decreases the chances for certain diseases. Due to the risk of pyometra (a life-threatening uterine infection that can occur in up to 50% of older female Newfoundlands over their lifetime, according to data from Sweden where elective sterilizations are generally not performed), non-breeding females are often spayed between 15 months and two years of age. Males are generally neutered at roughly the same age to reduce the risk of testicular and other cancers. Gastropexy effectively prevents bloat and is often done at the same time as the sterilization procedure.

Signs of Proestrus and Estrus

Given the pros and cons of spay/neutering timing, you should speak with your veterinarian about how these risk factors interrelate for your Newf, her activity levels, and her lifestyle. If you are postponing spaying of a female pup, you need to know the signs and symptoms when she goes into heat. First, she will be in proestrus for seven days; she will not be interested in mating, but male dogs will be interested in her. In the second phase (estrus), she will be fertile for approximately nine days. Signs of proestrus and estrus are

- swollen vulva and bloody vaginal discharge during proestrus phrase
- increased moodiness, growling at humans, or picking fights with other dogs in the household, especially other unspayed female dogs
- decreased or increased interest in human interactions
- increased interest in roaming or getting out of the yard (to look for male dogs to mate with)

To ensure that your female does not get pregnant, Dr. Sarah Wooten, a veterinary with Chewy, recommends:

- **Watch her closely.** When a dog is in heat, her only thought is to breed, and she will often do whatever it takes to find a mate. It's important to always keep your Newf supervised or contained in a crate or other secure enclosure so that she cannot get out and another dog cannot get in. There have been reports of dogs climbing fences to escape and mate and even getting pregnant through chain-link fences, so make sure that enclosure is secure!

- **Keep male dogs away.** If you have male dogs that have not been neutered, they need to be kept separate from the female dog. It's best if you can board the male dogs or have them stay at another house during the heat cycle. If that's not an option, make sure two barriers (doors or gates) are always in place between the dogs.

- **Consult your vet in emergencies.** If your dog accidentally mates during her heat cycle, there is a "morning after" injection that will terminate an unwanted pregnancy.

- **Close the windows.** Male dogs can detect female dogs in heat from over a mile away. By closing the windows, you contain your Newf's "perfume" to the house.

- **Take caution with walks.** It's not recommended to take dogs in heat on walks because of the risk of attracting male dogs. If you must take your Newf out, make sure she is on a secure leash, and bring a spray bottle filled with water to ward off any would-be wooers.

Pet Insurance

Obtaining insurance to cover your Newf is recommended, and coverage should be in effect when you bring your puppy home, as any previous treatment is considered preexisting, and that diagnosis will be excluded from future coverage. VCA has insurance policies for both routine veterinary care and for emergency/specialty veterinary care; these costs can be enormous for this giant breed. An Australian study found none of the dogs presenting with bloat with pet insurance were euthanized compared with a 66 percent euthanization rate among the dogs without pet insurance. Because it is an emergency procedure, it is covered by insurance. You may want to confirm which pet insurance policies your veterinarian will accept. See the Resource chapter for additional information on pet insurance.

Photo Courtesy
of Katie Dolan

Obesity

Perhaps the biggest impediment to your Newf's longevity and overall health is becoming overweight or obese. Newfs have a lower metabolic rate than other breeds and so are at risk of being overfed. Various studies suggest 40 to 50% of dogs in the United States are overweight or obese. In effect, fat becomes much like another organ and induces inflammation, which contributes to other illnesses and to more orthopedic injuries. Newfs are big dogs that are known to be sensitive to certain anesthesia. Being obese already puts a strain on a dog's heart and lungs, and when placed under anesthesia, the dog's already stressed heart and lungs will have to work even harder.

Of course, exercise helps reduce weight gain. Working Newfoundlands are generally fitter than dogs who are primarily pet companions, so consider a job for your Newf. See the nutrition chapter for additional resources on monitoring your dog's weight and preventing obesity.

> **"**
>
> *Most people are not feeding their dogs too much food; the culprit is treats. Put out a measuring cup on a kitchen table. Every time you give a dog a treat, put one in the cup. It's like picking blueberries: one for me, one for the cup. At the end of the day, check and see how many treats are in the cup. The treats are high calorie, often 1.5 times the equivalent amount of dog food. You are therefore supplementing your Newf's dog food with 10 mini meals every day.*
>
> CLYDE DUNPHY, DVM
> *Chair of the Newfoundland Club of America Charitable Trust*
>
> **"**

Vaccines

The appropriate vaccination schedule for dogs and whether to take titers before additional vaccinations is another area where people of goodwill disagree. Core vaccines are rabies (schedule based on state laws), canine parvovirus, canine distemper, canine adenovirus, and leptospirosis. Most veterinarians recommend a two-to-three week break between a rabies vaccination and a distemper vaccination.

Rabies: The rabies virus, which infects the central nervous system, manifests in dogs with excessive drooling, anxiety, and hallucinations. It is so deadly and highly contagious that nearly every state has established vaccination requirements.

Canine Distemper: This virus, which is spread by airborne droplets or sharing of dog bowls or toys, causes sneezing, coughing, gastrointestinal issues, and, in many cases, death. There is currently no cure for canine distemper.

HELPFUL TIP
Veterinary Specialists & Online Resources

Anesthesiology: https://acvaa.org
Behavior: https://avsab.org
Dentistry: www.avdc.org
Dermatology: www.acvd.org
Internal Medicine: www.acvim.org
Nutrition: www.acvn.org
Ophthalmology: www.acvo.com
Radiology: www.acvr.ucdavis.edu
Surgery: www.acvs.org
Theriogenology (Reproduction): https://www.theriogenology.org

Canine Adenovirus: The virus is spread via feces or contaminated fluids from infected dogs and may be present in a recovered dog for at least six months. Adenovirus causes infectious hepatitis in dogs, a serious liver disease that can be fatal in about 10-30 percent of cases.

Parvovirus: The virus is highly contagious and affects the gastrointestinal system, causing severe dehydration. An entire litter of puppies can become ill in a very short period of time.

Leptospirosis: The leptospirosis bacteria, which is found in soil and water, can cause stiffness, lethargy, kidney failure, fever, and vomiting. Antibiotics can be used to treat the disease, but preventative vaccines are recommended. The bacteria, which can also infect humans, appears to be on the increase, with hot spots including Texas, California, Oregon, and Appalachian Mountain states. Deciduous forest cover and high annual precipitation rates are associated with a higher incidence of leptospirosis disease in canines.

Researchers such as Dr. Jean Dodds suggest vaccinations can be avoided or minimized by taking titers to establish the dog's antibody levels before giving an additional vaccine. See this book's reference information to learn more about Dr. Dodds' work. Be sure to keep records of your dog's care and vaccinations. Increasingly, veterinary practices are creating patient portals with online access to dogs' records.

Fleas, Ticks, Heartworm, and Other Parasites

Untreated external parasites, including fleas, ticks, mites, ringworm, and lice, are vectors for disease and can be painful for your pet. Tiny mites, which burrow into a dog's skin or ears, will appear as dried blood like coffee grounds, while lice invade the skin and fur of a dog. Ringworm is a fungus that creates a ring on the dog's skin that can be treated with a fungal cream. A new strain of Rickettsia, a tick-borne bacterium, recently surfaced in southern states but, fortunately, can be treated with antibiotics (Kerns, 2022). Some pet owners and integrative veterinary medicine specialists may recommend herbal options and alternatives, while many owners use the standard medications available through their veterinarians.

Many breeders recommend using a lint brush on your dog as soon as you come indoors from an adventure where there might be ticks. The brush will remove hard-to-see ticks from your dog's coat before the ticks embed themselves in the skin. In addition, your yard can be sprayed for ticks, or you can try tick boxes. Field mice are coated with a tick deterrent when they run through the boxes and bring back the cotton balls to nests, thereby killing any ticks.

Internal parasites include:

- **Heartworm,** which is spread by mosquito bites, and is the most serious internal parasite as heartworm affects the dog's heart and lungs. It is treatable but should be prevented. Heartworm medication is generally given throughout the year in most parts of the United States. Testing should always be done before starting heartworm medication.

- **Hookworm** causes anemia and can be detected by fecal sample.

- **Tapeworms,** which can cause weight loss and intestinal blockages, can be treated with medications.

- **Roundworm,** which can retard growth in puppies, is evident in the dog's stool and can be treated with a dewormer.

- **Whipworm** invades the dog's intestines, causing digestive problems and fatigue. Deworming works, but the treatment often must be repeated every few months.

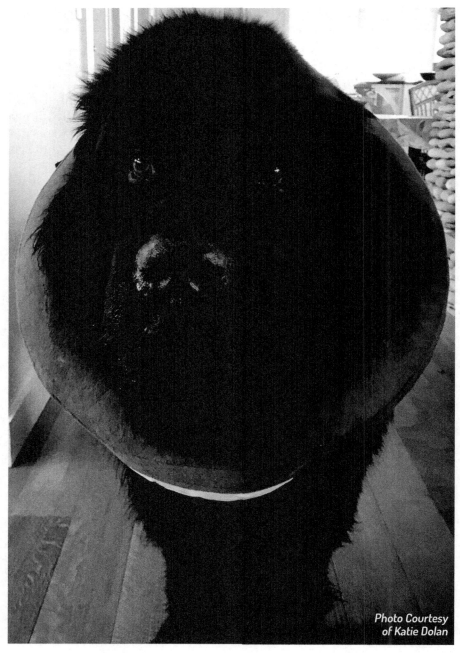

Photo Courtesy
of Katie Dolan

Blue wearing inflatable collar to prevent chewing on incisions post-surgery

Veterinary Specialties

At some point, you may need to consult a veterinary specialist for your dog. See information about the national associations for various specialties. You may also want to go directly to one of the 32 veterinary teaching schools in the United States (or the five Canadian and 16 international veterinary schools).

I'll share a quick story about Blue and the great orthopedic care he received at the Cummings School of Veterinary Medicine at Tufts. (Full disclosure: I'm on the school's board of advisors). When he was a year old, Blue needed surgery to remove bone fragments from both elbows. As a follow-up, he was evaluated by the Cummings Orthopedic service, and we learned he would likely need surgery on both hips. We gave him plenty of exercise and kept him thin; when we returned for a pre-op evaluation a few months later, we received the great news that his hips had stabilized and no surgery was needed. We did not neuter him and kept him in good shape. He had an undescended testicle that needed to be removed to prevent cancer, but again the orthopedic service recommended a conservative strategy, and Blue's other testicle was left intact. Happily, Blue is still doing well at 10 years of age. Our only challenge now is to manage unspayed Willow and intact Blue in the same house when she goes into heat.

Common Accidents

The most common canine accidents include foreign body ingestion, insect stings, bite wounds, torn nails, tooth injury, drug toxicity or overdose, eye trauma, poisoning or plant toxicity, muscle or joint trauma, and back injuries. The American Red Cross book entitled *Dog First Aid* may be a good resource. Also, know the location of emergency veterinarian services in your area and keep your veterinarian's phone number handy.

Top Dog Poisons

As noted in the discussion of puppy-proofing, dogs frequently get into the following toxic substances:

- **Over-the-counter medications** such as Tylenol, Advil, and Aleve, as well as some herbal and nutraceutical products, can be deadly to dogs.
- **Prescription medications for people** are dangerous to dogs.

- **People foods such as onions and garlic,** as well as beverages that are perfectly safe for people, can be dangerous and sometimes fatal for dogs.

- **Alcohol:** Symptoms of alcohol poisoning in animals are like those in people and may include vomiting, breathing difficulties, coma and, in severe cases, death.

- **Chocolate:** Chocolate contains caffeine and theobromine, both of which are toxic for dogs.

- **Macadamia nuts:** Dogs may suffer from a series of symptoms, including weakness, overheating, and vomiting, after consumption of macadamia nuts.

- **Grapes and raisins:** Experts aren't sure why, but these fruits can induce kidney failure in dogs. Even a small number may cause problems in some dogs.

- **Xylitol:** This sweetener is found in many products, including sugar-free gum and candy. It causes a rapid drop in a dog's blood sugar, resulting in weakness, seizures, and liver failure.

- **Other foods** to keep away from your pet include tomatoes, mushrooms, and most seeds and nuts.

For advice on accidental ingestion of these poisons, call the ASPCA Poison Control Center at (888) 426-4435.

First Aid for Dogs

Hopefully, you will never confront the need for emergency treatment of your dog. However, being able to manage your dog during an emergency can help in a stressful situation, so prior training and socialization are important. You might also want to take a course in Canine CPR and learn specifics of the American Red Cross emergency techniques. Here are the basics of Canine CPR:

1. **Check for breathing and a heartbeat...**Check to see if the dog is breathing and check for a heartbeat. If you do not see your dog's chest moving and cannot find a heartbeat, begin CPR with chest compressions. Position your dog so he is lying on his right side and work on his left side (closer to the heart).

2. **Give chest compressions...**For deep-chested dogs, place the heel of one hand over the widest part of the chest and place your other hand directly over the first hand. Then, push hard and push fast at a rate of

100–120 compressions per minute, compressing one-third to half the width of your pet's chest. Make sure the chest comes back fully (recoils) before compressing again. Perform 30 chest compressions.

3. **Give rescue breaths...**To give rescue breaths, gently close your pet's mouth and extend her neck to open the airway. Cover your pet's nose with your mouth and exhale until you see the chest rise. Give a second rescue breath.

4. **Continue CPR...**Continue giving CPR with a cycle of 30 chest compressions and two rescue breaths until your dog begins breathing again on her own.

5. **Check again for breathing and a heartbeat...**Briefly check for breathing and a heartbeat every two minutes.

6. **Get help...**Continue CPR until you reach a veterinary hospital.

Key items for a canine first aid kit for your car include documentation of vaccinations for your dog, scissors, tweezers, gauze bandages, hydrogen peroxide, blanket, water, washcloth, medical tape, sterile eyewash, and your veterinary's name/contact information.

Disaster Preparations

You should have an emergency plan for a disaster, including out-of-state contacts, extra bags of food and water in the car, identification, and cash. The Newfoundland Club of America has an excellent Disaster Preparedness Checklist for Pets.

CHAPTER 11
Grooming

> **"**
>
> *Most people are not prepared for the intense grooming required by a Newfoundland. I always suggest that people take their Newf to a groomer every six to eight weeks. If one chooses to groom a Newf at home, it is a good idea to get lessons. YouTube has some good videos where one can learn about the necessary tools and how to groom. Newfs should be brushed out at least once per week.*
>
> AMY CUTLER DAVIS
> *Birchbark Newfoundlands*
>
> **"**

Time, trimming, tangles, tools, training, treats: these words summarize the grooming of Newfoundlands. Their double coat, which makes them buoyant and is protective, should not be shaved unless there is a health problem. Newfs shed and have tons of hair. They need to be brushed daily and must be thoroughly brushed at least once a week. If you are relaxed and enjoy the process, your dog will too, and it is a great way to bond with your Newfoundland.

Overview

When grooming, remove the loose undercoat, but remember that the undercoat provides buoyancy while swimming and protection from extremes in weather. The coat should not be matted, but a bit of under-coat serves a purpose. For full professional grooms, locating a groomer with experience grooming the breed is helpful. Check with regional club members, your breeder or rescue chair, or other Newf families. Regional clubs often offer grooming seminars to teach new Newfy families how to groom and care for their dogs. Finally, be prepared to clean the lint filter in your clothes dryer every time. It will be full of soft Newfy hair.

Photo Courtesy
of Jessica Hoffman

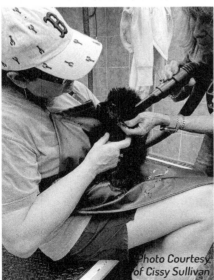

Photo Courtesy
of Cissy Sullivan

Photo Courtesy
of Katie Dolan

*Willow with grooming tools, from left to right:
Pin brush, Rake, Slicker brush, Steel comb*

Every breeder and groomer interviewed for this book emphasized the importance of routine grooming for this double-coated, shaggy breed. Puppies should be introduced to being touched on their paws and bodies, to the grooming experience, and to high-velocity (not human!) hairdryers early in their lives. Puppies should be brushed daily and bathed once a month. Much of grooming is preparation for the light trim of ears, feet, and feathers. A careful comb out before the bath and careful drying of the dog are the critical first steps. In general, a bath every five weeks (when not going to shows) and daily grooming/full brushing twice a week or a visit to a professional groomer every six weeks are recommended. Special breed considerations include changing the grooming regimen for older dogs and the impact of nutrition on the dog's coat.

The best grooming tip I can give is to invest in a high-velocity dryer and a sturdy grooming table. Even if you are taking your Newf to a professional groomer, you will want to be able to groom between appointments. Keeping your Newfoundland dry and mat free helps prevent skin issues such as hot spots. You'll need a good wide-tooth comb and slicker brush to maintain the coat. Learning to line comb is extremely important. There are videos on YouTube demonstrating this. In addition to caring for the coat, don't forget to clean the ears and trim the nails. Cleaning ears after swimming can help reduce the chances of getting an ear infection, and keeping nails trimmed and the hair between the pads trimmed helps prevent slipping.

SHEILA MALLINSON
Kodiak Acres

The Bath

Because Newf coats are water-resistant, it takes time to get a dog wet enough to apply shampoo. Do not bathe more frequently than every five weeks, as too much bathing will reduce needed oils. Put cotton balls into your dog's ears to keep water out of them. Wash the body first and then the head. Use a tearless shampoo like "So Gentle" and wash the ears twice. Thorough drying of the skin is essential, or an increase in the likelihood of

Photo Courtesy of Katie Dolan

chronic skin infections exists. Just like humans, Newfs can get athlete's foot, and so their paws need to be dried. Many Newfy fanciers and professional groomers recommend the K9 III dryer.

My best grooming tip is not to let Newfs get matted. This will require brushing at least twice a week, paying special attention to areas such as behind the ears, under arms, and groin areas. Using the right equipment is very important and should be discussed with your breeder. To keep skin healthy and coat in optimum condition, Newfs should be bathed once a month and completely blown dry with a high-velocity dog or cattle dryer. The high-velocity dryer is a must for this breed, and a grooming table will save your back.

CECE GUYATT
Trinity Cove Newfoundlands

Basic Grooming Tips from Becky Reynnells

Becky notes her background in both dogs and photography helps her while grooming; she has a picture in her mind of the perfect Newf and grooms a dog to create that image. She has been raising and grooming dogs for decades. Here are some of her recommendations:

- **Specific Tools and Products:** A guard comb, curved scissors, thinning shears, rake, and slicker brush are the basic tools for grooming a Newf. Becky recommends the following grooming sprays: OMG by Plush Puppy, Ice on Ice by Christopher C, or Quicker Slicker by Nature's Specialty. Use the rake to remove the loose undercoat.

- **Approach:** Work against the grain back to front and then reverse; use a good-quality shampoo, towel dry, and then blow dry completely.

- **Coats and Nutrition:** Each dog is an individual. Some have beautiful coats with no adjustments to their diet, while others may benefit from supplements or a dietary change. Speak to your veterinarian if you think your dog's coat is dull.

- **Teeth and Mouth:** Giving your Newf marrow bones to gnaw on will help remove tartar and keep her teeth in good shape, especially if you apply a tartar dissolving gel on a periodic basis. Once the dog is older, dental cleanings may be required. Removing debris and excess moisture from your dog's jowls is the best way to keep them healthy. Speak with your veterinarian about the best products for cleaning your dog's jowls.

Photo Courtesy of Katie Dolan

Veterinarians will often recommend safe-to-use medicated wipes, or they can recommend a product that you can get at a local dog store.

- **Ears:** If the dog's ears are healthy, leave them alone except for once-a-week cleaning. However, many dogs that come in for grooming have infections that should be treated by a veterinarian. If your dog is going to be swimming, use an ear wash both before and after the swim.

- **Eyes:** If you see behavioral changes while grooming your Newfoundland, check the eyes for cataracts. There are surgical options for dogs who develop cataracts. Some breeders check the eyes beginning at four months of age and for the duration of the dog's breeding career, as cataracts can be genetic.

- **Shaving:** Shaving younger dogs for a "summer cut" is generally not a good idea, as the dog could develop "clipper alopecia," where his guard hairs do not grow back. Of course, if a dog is heavily matted, shaving may be the only option.

Photo Courtesy of Gary Baldwin

Advanced Grooming Seminar with Penny Shubert

Through the local Newfoundland club, I joined a grooming clinic with icon Penny Shubert. She has groomed thousands of dogs across the country and helped prepare Josh for his win at Westminster. She also does bird carving, so she can look at an ungroomed Newf and create a groomed dog emulating the breed standard.

Penny groomed a patient Grand Champion dog named Navy with entertaining commentary on what she was doing and why. Her advice to novice groomers: "Hair is a renewable resource, so keep practicing with your dog."

Other highlights and fun tidbits from Penny:

- Groomers use lingo for the various parts of a dog. The back of the head and shoulders is the turtle; the front of the dog is a buffalo; the rear of the dog becomes the fenders; and the lower back legs are the knee socks.

- "Line combing" is a technique where the dog's coat is parted down to its skin using a metal comb and then combed out, small half-inch sections at a time.

- Start with the underside of the dog, which is likely to be the most matted, then the belly, under the armpits, and the "pooper end of the dog." Clip the hair between the pads. Long fur on the pads can cause the dog to slip and can cause infections.

- If a Newf intensely blows its coat due to pregnancy or a medical condition, it will take three years for the fur on the tail to completely grow back and two years for the feathering on the legs to grow back.

- Be careful when standing directly behind a Newf. As Penny reports from experience, "They can kick like mules."

- Before grooming, look at the dog and see what he needs to look great in the show ring. You'll generally groom to make the head appear larger since a Newf head doesn't finish growing until age five.

It was a great seminar, and new Newf owners would enjoy attending a future session with Penny. (In addition to attending a grooming clinic, new Newf owners may want to look at the Newf rescue website (http://www.newfrescue.com/grooming-tips) for an illustrated guide by Iwonna Salak of Logrus Newfoundlands in Italy.)

Professional Groomers

When sending your dog to a professional groomer, you might want to include a pic of a Newf that has a nice shape. Try to find a groomer that has experience with Newfoundlands.

Another Benefit of Grooming

When Bella was young, we'd drive up to Todd's Point in Greenwich to join the Bernese Mountain Dog Walking group. She romped on the beach and in the waves amidst burly Bernese, Mastiffs, and other generously sized canines. I was repeatedly asked, "What's his name?" The next time we traveled up to the beach, I left the groomer's two pink bows on her ears to ensure fellow beachgoers knew my big black dog was female.

CHAPTER 12

Newfoundlands Working and in the Show Ring

Thinking. Teamwork. Training. Tenacity. These words describe the process of working with a Newfoundland. One of the pleasures of owning a Newf is watching her joy as she works, whether in therapy, draft, water rescue, obedience, agility, or conformation. Newfy owners rave about the special bond created by a canine-human team working together. Participating in these activities keeps your dog mentally and physically active. It also provides a great way for Newfy owners to meet others who are passionate about the breed. This chapter, which draws heavily on the great materials on the Newfoundland Club of America website, provides an overview of ways you can work with your dog and stories from Newfoundland owners who have shared these bonding experiences with their dogs.

Versatile Newf

The Newfoundland Club of America established the designation of Versatile Newfoundland to encourage and recognize beautiful representatives of the breed who continue to exhibit the breed's historic and natural working abilities. To be recognized as a Versatile Newfoundland, a dog must earn an AKC championship, an AKC Companion Dog obedience title, an NCA Water Rescue Dog title, and an NCA Draft Dog title. Approximately 20 dogs per year achieve this prestigious award.

"

For all training, whether for show training or obedience or other performance, one must find a way to get and hold a dog's attention. This must be rewarded with something of value to the dog. As I begin training, my dogs will always work for food. Gradually I will replace food treats with verbal praise or a tossed favorite toy. However, as I teach new commands, I find that my dogs' brains are closely connected to their appetites. Treats might be small tidbits of meat or cheese or even just kibble. I repurchased a two-year-old male who would only respond to pieces of bagel, so that was how this boy earned his Versatile Newf title. As I start with a baby puppy, I will walk on a loose lead and click with my tongue for attention. That click is rewarded with food. Later that click can be rewarded with food and "Good Dog" and later with only "Good Dog."

I find that most beginner trainers try to train in sentences. I use only simple words. Come, Sit, Down, Stay, Take, Help, Back, Here, Find, and Jump commands can accomplish almost everything a dog needs to do to become an accomplished performance dog and a dog that is a pleasure to live with. It is a lot easier for a dog to comprehend than a string of words such as "Rover, take this knotted rope, hold it, carry it out to the person calling, good boy, good boy, now, go around him, go around, and then come back to shore, come here." Instead, "Take. Go Help" should work. "Take" to me and my dog means to grasp whatever I offer and hold it. "Help" means to go to the person who is calling for help wherever he might be calling, in the water or land or in a boat.

BETTY MCDONNELL,
Kilyka Newfoundlands
Betty has trained 25 of her dogs (Newfs and Norwich Terriers) to Utility Dog and Versatility titles.

"

Conformation

In conformation, the judge evaluates each dog against the breed standard. Under the AKC system, points are awarded to winning dogs based on the number of dogs defeated in several trials, and a dog receives a championship after earning a total of 15 points. There are seven classes per breed in American Kennel Club dog shows:

1. **Puppy:** divided between 6–9 months and 9–12 months.

2. **12–18 Months** (those that fall in this age range are eligible).

3. **Novice:** Dogs over six months old are eligible if they have not won any points yet, have not yet won three first-place prizes in this class, and have not won first prizes in the Bred-By-Exhibitor, American-bred, or Open classes.

Photo Courtesy of Katie Dolan

4. **Amateur Owner-Handler:** The owner exhibits the dog and has not received funds for showing any other dog.

Photo Courtesy of Katie Dolan

5. **Bred-By-Exhibitor:** The handler is an owner and a breeder of record.

6. **American-Bred:** For dogs conceived in the US.

7. **Open:** Any dog over six months old can enter this class. Champions are not allowed in any of the other classes and are only permitted to enter this class, although in most cases, they skip the class competition entirely and are entered directly in Best of Breed.

At the National, separate classes also include Veterans (7 to 9 and over 9) and Open classes for both Black and Other than Black Newfoundlands. Generally, there are two AKC-sponsored all-breed events in various parts of the country each year. You can find a listing of shows on the AKC website (akc.org).

Water Rescue

In a Newfoundland water test, the bond between dog and handler is front and center as the dog's ability to save a human life is displayed, and hours of intense training are evident. The WRD and WRDX water tests show the unique traits of the breed. A Newfoundland's large stature, powerful muscles, waterproof coat, and webbed feet all enable the dog to stroke through the water with speed and endurance to rescue a drowning person. The advanced test for elite working dogs includes searching for an abandoned boat and returning it to land; rescuing multiple victims and returning them to a boat; rescue of an unconscious victim; a rescue of a victim under a capsized boat; delivering a line to shore from a stranded boat; and rescuing two drowning victims from behind a boat. Newfoundlands, with their oily coat, webbing between their toes, a tail that acts like a rudder, and an undercoat for buoyancy, are well designed for cold-water swimming.

Photo Courtesy of Patti Sutherland

> *Dwight and Christine Gorsuch believe their Newfoundlands are happier and healthier when busy with lots to do and much to think about and learn. Earning the Versatile Newf designation (achieving titles in Conformation, Obedience, Draft, and Water Rescue) keeps their dogs (and owners) active and thinking. Asked about surprises during the tests, Dwight says, "We train them until we think they are ready to pass, so on test day, we may be nervous, but we're confident. We had a dog (Cody) that had completed all the VN title components except for his Water Rescue Title. On test day, he was passing each exercise of the WRD test. On his final exercise, which was to jump from a boat to me in the water, he refused to jump. Cody never earned his VN. I'm sure many trainers have similar stories about things not going as planned when the dog just decides not to do something one day.*
>
> *I had a small puppy (Cassidy) that I taught to swim in our pool. I put a small life jacket on her, and we practiced her jumping from the pool deck and into my arms like you would do with a child. Cassidy got to be very proficient at that jump. As she got bigger, I backed up away from the pool's edge, and she jumped farther and farther toward me. One of the water rescue exercises requires an owner and dog to go out in a boat, then the owner jumps in and swims 10 feet away, and the dog is supposed to jump off the boat and 'rescue' its owner. Well, Cassidy jumped in but jumped right on top of me every time. With training, we eventually fixed this error, and I learned to implement the transition from pool to boat in a different way. Every dog is different, so you must be ready to try different techniques.*
>
> *Christine had a female who bonded to her, and I had a male who bonded with me. They were very close in age, and we raised them together, showed them together, did obedience classes together, and had a mini-family competition to see which dog would get its VN first. The lead went back and forth; first it was the female who had more titles, then it was the male. The dogs both ultimately received their VNs, but Christine's female got there first."*
>
> **DWIGHT GORSUCH**
> *Bear N Mind Newfoundlands*

Photo Courtesy
of Cissy Sullivan

Cissy~PictureThis

Draft

The Newfoundland Club of America Draft Tests are a series of exercises designed to develop and demonstrate the natural abilities of purebred Newfoundland dogs and teamwork skills. The Newfoundland has historically functioned as a draft dog in various capacities, and the performance of these exercises is intended to demonstrate skills resulting both from natural ability and training. The goal of each handler is to maintain control while encouraging the dog's natural independence; together, they demonstrate teamwork. Since a dog can perform draft work only in cooperation with a person, each handler must demonstrate an understanding of draft work with the dog's ability, training, and equipment. When the Guinness Book of World Records maintained hauling statistics, a Newfoundland held the title for greatest proportional weight hauled: 52 times the weight of the dog.

Obedience

Obedience trials demonstrate the dog's ability to follow specified routines in the obedience ring and emphasize the usefulness of the dog as a companion to humankind. In 2018, there were 118,316 entries in AKC obedience trials. A variety of obedience titles can be earned, starting with the title of Companion Dog, and progressing all the way up to an Obedience Trial Champion. The dog and its handler are asked to perform a variety of activities, from heeling on a leash to staying to a recall.

"

Newfs like to please, it's true, but they do not like to respond to a command that makes no sense to them. This attribute is probably best understood with a story. I was participating in a draft test with my Newfy Cyrus. Drafting is an activity in which a Newfy pulls a cart. The draft test has four major parts, all performed off lead. One part is the maneuvering course with basic commands. The maneuvering course, among numerous challenges, takes the dog into a thicket that requires the Newfy to back up and then route itself around the impassable area. Cyrus stopped and planted his four feet before entering the thicket. He could see that he could not get through and knew he would have to back up the cart to avoid the tangled greenery. He would not move forward. He refused the command to go into the thicket. He stepped to his right and pulled the cart forward to the open area so that he could continue without entering the thicket on the unobstructed course. We failed the draft test then and there.

The challenge Cyrus and I faced then and in our future attempts to pass the draft test was finding a way to convince a thinking Newfy he needed to just follow what I was asking him to do...even if what I was asking him to do did not make sense to him. After eight different draft test failures, Cyrus acquiesced, and we finally earned the title. So, when training a Newfy, vary the routine so that it's not predictable.

JUDITH M. ZIFFER
Sandy Cove Newfoundlands

"

Therapy Dog

A Newf makes a great therapy dog; people want to pet the dog's shiny coat and enjoy its gentle disposition. A variety of organizations around the country offer certifications for therapy dogs. Several years ago, the AKC issued standards for therapy dogs, and the qualifying organizations are listed on the AKC website. Various AKC therapy dog titles are based on the number of visits completed by the dog.

In addition, NewfTherapy (see https://newfietherapy.org) is an organization providing Animal-Assisted Activities (AAA) and Animal-Assisted Therapy (AAT), primarily with giant-breed Newfoundland dogs, to veterans, military families, first responders, health care workers, and people overcoming

Photo Courtesy
of Karen Steinrock

> *Every family's Newfoundland is a therapy, assistance, or service dog to some extent. When you come home after a particularly dreadful day at work, your Newf lays his head on your knee and tells you it'll be better soon. When a pair of balled-up socks falls out of the overloaded hamper you are carrying up the stairs, that Newf will pick them up and bring them to you. When your arthritis flares up and you can't hoist yourself out of the couch, your Newfoundland will hold rock-still, letting you grab on and pull yourself to your feet. However, there are Newfoundlands that take that genetic calling to a much higher level. They serve in hospitals or schools, care facilities or nursing homes. They visit elementary schools, libraries, museums and summer camps, and the entertaining programs they present demonstrate their helpful skills to eager audiences.*
>
> **JUDI ADLER**
> *Sweetbay Newfoundlands*

dog visits have been provided. One of the people served by this program writes: "PTSD is a mental illness that is silent but always there, hiding in the background, just waiting to surface, through flashbacks or days battling depression. Combine that with a life-threatening illness and some days seem insurmountable. Wrapping my arms around a massive bear-like dog manages to bring peace in a way that medicine just doesn't accomplish. When I'm surrounded by these joyful animals, anything seems possible. I forget about fear and pain, and I'm able to live in the day, full of joy."

> *My Newfoundland Rufus was a well-bred Newf, far more excited about therapy visits than swimming. Although Rufus failed the simple "guppy test" at a regional water event, he passed a challenging test for state certification to visit patients at Harrisburg State Hospital. Many of the patients suffered from schizophrenia and other psychiatric disorders. One day Rufus and I were making our rounds, and a nurse came running, saying. "We need Rufus right now!" A young woman strapped to a gurney was screaming in terrible distress. Rufus gently nudged and calmed this poor woman within five minutes. I did nothing other than handle the end of the leash. He did all the work. To this day, I still hear from family members who remember his visits.*
>
> *Rufus also calmed patients at a local nursing home. I can picture "Bill" sitting on his bed in a plaid shirt and suspenders, head down, and uncommunicative with anyone since his admission a week beforehand. In fact, he hadn't spoken a word. The nurses all knew Rufus, if anyone, could bring him out of his shell. Rufus calmly walked to Bill's bedside. After a moment, the 150-pound furry visitor, sensing acceptance, jumped up and sat quietly by Bill. Within seconds, Bill was hugging and talking to him. That connection was so strong that even I was stunned, as we had done therapy work for years. Bill asked the nurse and me to leave the room so he could be alone with Rufus, saying, "You out. HE can stay." We watched from the hallway, but everyone knew Rufus was the dog for this job. After that, Bill was on our regular visiting list.*
>
> **KAREN STEINROCK**
> *Newfoundland owner*

Freestyle

You and your partner take your place on the floor. Your choreographed routine flashes through your mind. You take a couple of deep breaths. You look into your partner's eyes for reassurance. The familiar music starts, and off you go. This scenario may suggest pairs figure skating or ballroom dancing, but what if I told you that your partner is your dog? Canine freestyle is a blend of traditional obedience and nontraditional "dance" movements performed to music. Teamwork between dog and handler is essential. Freestyle is a wonderful way to demonstrate your dog's intelligence, skills, beauty, and fun-loving spirit.

Photo Courtesy of Paul Pribula

> " Canine musical freestyle, often called dancing with dogs, is a fun, tail-wagging sport based on obedience, tricks, and additional behaviors that your dog enjoys. It includes music, choreography, costuming, routine development, and showmanship. Freestyle is not just fun but also functional by keeping your dog mentally and physically active. Spinning, bowing, weaving (yes, Newfs can weave), and kicking all help to strengthen core muscles and maintain flexibility throughout your dog's life. You and your dog can compete for titles, perform demos at events, or just have fun in your own backyard. "
>
> LAUREL RABSCHUTZ
> *Freestyle Fan*

Search and Rescue

Search and rescue is the term that is applied to the act of looking for a missing or lost person. Search and rescue dogs are trained to assist in the location of missing or lost persons. Each search and rescue dog handler

Photo Courtesy of Katie Dolan

decides how their dogs will find people, whether it be tracking, trailing, or air-scenting. Air-scenting means the dogs do not need a scent article to begin their search. The dogs are taught to scan the air current for any human scent. Tracking/trailing dogs are scent discriminating. This means they are given a scent article and will search for and follow that specific scent. Most search dog groups have dogs that do all or some of the following: wilderness searches, urban searches, water searches, avalanche searches, disaster searches (after tornadoes, earthquakes, mudslides, rockslides, building collapses, or multi-car crashes.), and cadaver searches. Experts estimate that a single trained search and rescue dog, under excellent conditions, can be as effective as 25 trained human ground searchers in locating a missing person within a given period of time. Dogs possess up to 300 million olfactory receptors in their noses compared with the 6 million receptors in humans.

Tracking and Nosework

Tracking is a sport version of search and rescue work. To earn a basic tracking title (TD), the dog must follow a stranger's scent 30 minutes after the stranger walks a predetermined zigzag course, then leaves a glove carrying his scent about a third of a mile away from the start. The dog works in harness on a 40-foot lead, with the handler following behind. AKC scent work is based on the task of working detection dogs to locate a scent and communicate to the handler that the scent has been found. Detection is done in a variety of environments and often during changing conditions. Scent work is a positive, challenging activity that allows dogs the opportunity to use their strongest natural sense in a way that is fun and engaging. Order a copy of the AKC Tracking Regulations and find a tracking club in your area. Most trackers are happy to help you get started, and you may be able to join them when they track their own dogs.

Rally

AKC Rally is a sport in which dog and handler complete a course designed by the rally judge. The judge tells the handler to begin, and dog and handler proceed at a brisk pace through a course of designated stations (10–20, depending on the level). Each of these stations has a sign providing instructions regarding the next skill that is to be performed. The dog and handler team moves continuously at a brisk but normal pace, with the dog under control at the handler's left side. The handler is permitted to talk with her dog throughout the course.

Photo Courtesy
of Gary Baldwin

Tricks

Do More With Your Dog (DMYD) is the world's leading trick dog program. There are two ways to earn AKC titles—test with an approved evaluator in person or via video or submit your DMYD Title directly to the AKC. For all levels, 10 tricks from the AKC-approved list for that level will be performed. The difficulty of tricks and the proficiency increases as the titling level increases. Treats are allowed as reinforcement at all levels and can be used as lures in some beginner tricks.

Agility

Agility is a growing dog sport, with over one million entries to the AKC's program each year. Dogs race against a clock as they navigate an obstacle course with strong concentration and speed. Whether you just want to have fun exercising with your dog or want to go further and enter an agility competition, get ready for a fast-paced, rewarding experience.

> *There is a reason light-boned, nimble dogs, such as the Border Collie, are the norm for the sport. Agility equipment and courses are the same for all breeds (except for the jump heights) and are designed for the "average" dog. We all know Newfs are far from average! A large, heavy-boned dog such as the Newfoundland is at a disadvantage when it comes to negotiating courses with tight turns (those darn laws of physics get in the way). Newfs must learn to run in a crouch through the tunnels. They don't have any margin for error when crossing the dog walk or the teeter, while jumping off the A-frame from above the contact zone is more like a big step than a jump. Dropped bars were (and still are) our nemesis. Gus can easily clear a 28" obedience jump from a complete standstill two feet in front of the jump, but I'm convinced that sometimes he can't be bothered with picking up his feet. Let's face it; knocking into a jump bar is just no big deal when you're the size of a Newf.*
>
> JENNI LOTT
> *Agility and Newfoundland Fan*

CHAPTER 13
Holidays

Fireworks Fears. Holiday hubbub. Trash temptations. These are the watchwords when it comes to holidays with our Newfoundlands. The holidays are busy times of the year, and household routines are often disrupted.

Overview

If you're hosting guests, ask them to help keep an eye on your dogs to make sure they don't escape. Place notes on exit doors and on gates to remind everyone to be vigilant. Make sure your Newf is equipped with identification tags with up-to-date information. Talk with your veterinarian about microchipping. This simple procedure can greatly improve your chances of getting your dog back if she is lost. Many Newf breeders send their puppies to forever homes with a microchip in place. Be sure your Newf is easily identified as yours by a collar with tags or other identification. We've found personalized collars embroidered with the dog's name and my cell phone

Photo Courtesy of Katie Dolan

number (see photo) work well. I have received telephone calls or texts telling me Blue's whereabouts on the adjacent beach when someone has left the garden gate ajar.

The American Veterinary Medical Association website (https://www. avma.org) offers detailed advice on taking care of pets during various holidays. Here are some suggestions relevant for Newfoundland owners:

Easter Dangers

In addition to protecting the chocolate bunnies from your dog, be sure to put away any fake grass, which can be dangerous if ingested.

Photo Courtesy of Jeana Yager

Fourth of July Fireworks

A study of over 13,000 Finnish dogs of various breeds found noise sensitivity, especially fear of fireworks, is the most common anxiety-related trait and occurs in one-third of canines (Howell et al. 2020). More pets go missing and are admitted to shelters around the Fourth of July than at any other time of the year. These festivities can be frightening and dangerous for animals. The heat is also a real risk during this summer holiday. And all those picnics and barbecues offer many foods that tempt counter-surfing pets.

My Bella once managed to escape our fenced yard, deciding to visit the next-door neighbors to help celebrate Independence Day. Unfortunately, they had just put a feast of delights on their wooden picnic table and had gone back inside to get cold drinks. We heard a commotion as they realized Bella had helped herself to much of the food. They were neighborly and laughed at the situation. Another time, Bella found discarded corn cobs in a firepit on the beach, ate them, and had an obstruction requiring emergency surgery.

Photo Courtesy of Katie Dolan

Fireworks can startle animals and cause them to run away. My Newfoundlands have never enjoyed fireworks but are far less nervous than our previous Golden Retriever, who hid in the bathtub if she heard distant fireworks. Keep your pets indoors, ideally in locations where firework noise is at a minimum (like the bathtub). Dogs might need a little extra help and encouragement finding a good spot to retreat. Keep windows and curtains closed to muffle sounds and see if lowering the lights, covering the crate, offering a new or favorite toy, or playing soothing music helps your Newf relax. We try to simply stay home with our dogs so that they don't get anxious.

Halloween Dangers

No tricks or human treats. Don't let your pets get into the Halloween candy, especially if it contains chocolate or xylitol (a common sugar substitute found in sugar-free candies and gum).

Make sure your pet is properly identified in case she escapes through the open door while you're distracted by trick-or-treaters, and keep lit candles, jack-o'-lanterns, glow sticks, and jewelry far from your pets. If your pet

Photo Courtesy of Katie Dolan

is wary of strangers, put her in another room during trick-or-treating hours or provide her with a safe hiding place.

December Holidays

Nothing can spoil a family holiday gathering like an emergency trip to the veterinary clinic. Be sure to know the route to a 24/7 emergency veterinary clinic before an emergency occurs. Talk with your veterinarian in advance to find out where you might need to take your dog. Keep these numbers posted in an easy-to-find location:

- Your veterinarian's clinic phone number
- 24/7 emergency veterinary clinic (if different)
- ASPCA Poison Control Hotline: 1-888-426-4435 (A fee may apply.)

Food

Keep people food away from pets. If you want to share holiday treats with your Newf, make or buy treats formulated just for dogs. As noted in previous chapters, the following people foods are especially hazardous for pets and are listed as a holiday time reminder:

- **Chocolate** is an essential part of the holidays for many people, but it is toxic to dogs and cats. Although the toxicity can vary based on the type of chocolate, the size of your pet, and the amount ingested, it's safer to consider all chocolate off-limits for pets.
- **Other sweets and baked goods** also should be kept out of reach. Not only are they often too rich for pets, but xylitol, an artificial sweetener often found in baked goods, candy, and chewing gum, has been linked to liver failure and death in dogs. Nutmeg is also problematic.
- **Turkey and turkey skin**, sometimes even in small amounts, can cause a life-threatening condition known as pancreatitis.
- **Table scraps**, including gravy and meat fat, should be kept away from pets. Many foods that are healthy for people are poisonous to dogs, including onions, raisins, and grapes. During the holidays, when our own diets tend toward extra-rich foods, table scraps can be especially fattening and hard for animals to digest and can even cause pancreatitis.
- **Yeast dough** can cause problems for dogs, including painful gas and potentially dangerous bloating.

Signs of distress include sudden changes in behavior, depression, pain, vomiting, or diarrhea.

Decorating

Greenery, lights, and Christmas trees make the holidays festive, but they also pose risky temptations for our pets. With thanks to both the AVMA and my fellow writers of dog breed books from LPMedia, here's a list of things to think about with a Newf in your home:

- **Christmas trees** can tip over if pets climb on them or try to play with the lights and ornaments. Consider tying your tree to the ceiling or a doorframe using fishing line to secure it.

- **Water additives for Christmas trees** can be hazardous. Do not add aspirin, sugar, or anything to the water for your tree if you have pets in the house.

*Photo Courtesy
of Jessica Hoffman*

- **Ornaments** can cause hazards for pets. Broken ornaments can cause injuries, and ingested ornaments can cause intestinal blockages or even toxicity. Keep any homemade ornaments, particularly those made from salt dough or other food-based materials, out of reach of pets. Place fragile ornaments up higher on the tree so that they don't get knocked down by a large Newfy tail.

- **Tinsel and other holiday decorations:** These items can be tempting for pets to eat. Consuming them can cause intestinal blockages, sometimes requiring surgery. Breakable ornaments or decorations can also cause injuries.

- **Electric lights** can cause burns when a curious pet chews the cords. Cover cords with electrical tape.

- **Flowers and festive plants:** Amaryllis, mistletoe, balsam, pine, cedar, and holly are among the common holiday plants that can be dangerous and even poisonous to pets who decide to eat them. Poinsettias can be troublesome as well.

- **Candles** are attractive to pets. Never leave a pet alone in an area with a lit candle; it could result in a fire.

- **Potpourris** should be kept out of reach. Liquid potpourris pose risks because they contain essential oils and cationic detergents that can severely damage a pet's mouth, eyes, and skin. Solid potpourris could cause problems if eaten.

Holiday Parties

Visitors can upset pets, as can the noise and excitement of holiday parties. Even pets that aren't normally shy may become nervous in the hubbub of a holiday gathering. We usually let our Newfs greet early guests for 5-10 minutes (a little drool adds glamour to those black velvet pants) and then give them marrow bones in our bedroom. Other suggestions:

- **All pets** should have access to a comfortable, quiet place inside if they want to retreat. Make sure your dog has a room or crate somewhere away from the commotion, where your guests won't follow so that she can go anytime she wants to get away.

- **Inform your guests** ahead of time that you have pets or if other guests may be bringing pets to your house.

- **Guests with pets?** If guests ask to bring their own pets and you don't know how the pets will get along, you should either politely decline their request or plan to spend some time acclimating the pets to each other, supervising their interactions, monitoring for signs of a problem, and taking action to avoid injuries to pets or people.

- **Clear the food** from tables, counters, and serving areas when you are done using them, and make sure the trash gets put where your pet can't reach it. Dispose of carcasses and bones—and anything used to wrap or tie the meat, such as strings, bags, and packaging— in a covered, tightly secured trash bag placed in a closed trash container outdoors (or behind a closed, locked door).

- **Trash** also should be cleared away where pets can't reach it, especially sparkly ribbon and other packaging or decorative items that could be tempting for your pet to play with or consume.

Holiday Gift Ideas

All the precautions listed above may make me seem like the Grinch Who Stole Christmas or Ebeneezer Scrooge, so I'll wrap up this chapter (pun intended) with a few holiday gift ideas for Newfoundland people and their dogs.

Gifts for Newfs:

- Kongs and chew toys
- Agility equipment for backyard
- Training treats
- Personalized collar

Gifts for Newf People:

- For animal lovers of all ages, check out the *Bella, the Wildlife Ambassador* series, available on Amazon.com

- See newfielove.com, Newfs by Enchanted Designs Facebook page, or Black Paw Studio at https://www.blackpawstudio.com, Prairie Dog pottery www.prairiedogpottery.ca for clothing, painted holiday ornaments, and other gift ideas.

- For Newf books, search on Amazon.com or go to the NCA website
- Poop bags and leashes

Buying a Christmas puppy is not a great idea. Most reputable breeders avoid having litters before the holidays as they don't want to place a puppy in a home amid the holiday chaos.

CHAPTER 14

Traveling with Your Newf

> *Travel with your pup from an early age, and he will love a car ride. As he grows, you will need a ramp or steps for him to get in and out of your car safely unless you have a minivan. Newfs like cooler temperatures and love the movement of air. You can get a fan that plugs into the car and point it toward the dogs to keep the air flowing...Most of us purchase 'Newfmobiles,' which are usually minivans or SUVs.*
>
> MARY BYLONE,
> *Sea Worthy Newfoundlands*

Safely secured. Heat risk in cars. Planning. All watchwords for the road. Traveling with a Newf can be fun and rewarding. Newfs are generally very good travelers. Whenever our dogs see the suitcases out, notice dog food being packed, or detect the general bustle of preparations, they stick close, hoping to get out to the garage and wait for us to invite them into the car. Not all Newfs are like mine; some are fearful of getting into a vehicle and should first be taken on short trips in the car so they can get used to the experience.

It is best to secure your Newf either in a crate or a seat belt with a harness adapter to prevent her from becoming a dangerous projectile in an accident. According to an American Automobile Association study, 84% of dogs are not properly secured while traveling in the car. Never drive with your dog in the back of an open truck; over 100,000 dogs die each year from accidents in open trucks. And don't let your Newf hang her head out

Photo Courtesy of Katie Dolan

the window during car travel as flying bugs and debris can damage her delicate eyes. (The vast majority of canine eye injuries result from dog noses and muzzles sticking out car windows.) In addition, the temperatures in a vehicle rise very rapidly when the engine is shut off and no air conditioning is on. Many dogs have died when left unattended in a parked car. Newfs are particularly susceptible to heat, so never leave your dog in a car unattended.

Travel Gear

Many seasoned Newf travelers put their dogs in metal crates that are secured in the vehicle, while others use harnesses secured to the seat belts. In addition, a portable dog ramp or steps allows your Newf to get into and out of the car without putting stress on her joints. Newfs can be easily trained to use the ramp or steps. Another option is a hideaway step, which mounts to the bottom of a truck or large vehicle and swings out to create a step for humans and Newfs.

> ❝
>
> *The right vehicle is important. A smaller compact car prevents safe travel, as you need space for a secured crate. Pay attention to the height of an SUV as you may need to use stairs or ramps and train your Newfoundland to use them properly. It is very hard for a Newf to jump in and out of a vehicle and doing so can cause injury to the hip and elbow joints.*
>
> **KATIE STANKEY**
> *Bigluv Newfoundlands*
>
> ❞

General Newfy Travel Tips

- Have a leash readily available in case a quick or unexpected pit stop is necessary.

- If you will be traveling across national or international borders, you may need a certificate of health from an accredited veterinarian. (See Resource chapter.)

- Vans, minivans, and SUVs are great travel vehicles for big dogs. It is best if the vehicle has rear air conditioning to keep your Newf cool.

- Do some Internet research so you can bring along the name and number of a local veterinarian where you will be staying.

- Make certain your Newf is microchipped and that her name and your phone number are printed on her collar. When traveling, Newfs should always be kept on a lead, crated in hotels, and their excrement needs to be picked up and appropriately discarded.

- Bring a slobber towel, paper towels, and trash bags in case the dog gets car sick.

- Get your pup used to the car while she is young. Go to fun places, not just to the vet's or groomer's but also to the park, a local feed store, a pet store, or a coffee shop.

- Bring water from home when traveling so your dog doesn't get an upset stomach.

Hotels and Rentals

About 75% of hotels allow pets, according to a 2016 survey, and several major hotel chains are pet friendly. Call ahead and make reservations. More and more hotels are pet-friendly, but some may have dog weight restrictions that Newfs usually exceed. Add a "pets allowed" filter in your search for a hotel or rental to see options. I have had good luck emailing possible Airbnb rentals, even with listings that don't allow dogs, to get permission for my Newfoundlands to stay.

Photo Courtesy of Katie Dolan

Parks and Natural Areas

Roadtrippers is a great app for finding parks and natural spots to walk with your dog. Plug in your route and ask for the map to show you natural areas. I was surprised to find new places to stop on a cross-county route that we've driven several times. In addition, some of the national parks are surprisingly dog friendly, including Acadia in Maine (with 145 miles of hiking trails open to dogs), Shenandoah in West Virginia, Hot Springs in Arkansas, Mammoth Cave in Kentucky, the Petrified Forest in Arizona, and White Sands in New Mexico. For additional dog-friendly parks, go to https://roadtripppers. com/magazine/dog-friendly-national-parks.

Leaving Your Newf at Home

You also can leave your Newf at a boarding kennel or at home with a dog sitter. Some dogs are anxious in boarding kennels; try a short stay to see how your Newf reacts before scheduling a longer vacation or trip. In addition, stressed dogs are more likely to develop bloat, so make sure your Newf is happy in a boarding situation. You will have to show up-to-date vaccinations, including Bordetella, for your dog. Be sure to tell the boarding kennel about your dog's dietary needs, schedule, preferences, and quirks.

Photo Courtesy of Liz Hauser

Because we have two Newfoundlands (and because we spoil our dogs), it has generally been cheaper to find a sitter who will live in our home. We recently tried Trustedhousesitters.com, a website that matches people interested in house/dog sitting with people who have homes in attractive locations. We posted pictures of our dogs and house while the pet sitter described her dog-sitting experience and background. We were matched with a great sitter who was thrilled to play with our Newfs and worked remotely from our home in the mountains. Rover.com is a similar option, matching dog walkers and dog sitters with dog owners. Be sure to have written instructions for any pet sitter, with information on your veterinarian, feeding instructions, location of poop bags and leash, general schedule, medication instructions, and anything else that someone would want to know to care for your Newf like you do. Our dog sitter sent fun pics of the dogs as well.

Friends Visiting and Friends' Homes

With two large drooling Newfoundlands, we don't get frequent invitations to stay at other people's homes. When we do, however, it is very important to dog-proof our living space where possible. We put our toiletry kits and the dog food in a secure place and make sure the garbage cans are hidden away. We also make sure to arrive with plenty of time for the dogs to exercise, adjust to the new place, and settle in before we leave them in a hotel room or at a friend's home.

Our biggest issues with food stolen or medicine ingested have always been with friends who were unaccustomed to the Newfoundland proclivity to counter-surf. In addition to reminding people to put groceries away and close the pantry door, I put signs on bedroom doors reminding guests that our Newfs like to explore suitcases, so be sure to put away toiletries and medicines, put away food or snacks stored in suitcases, and shut the bedroom door firmly. It is very easy to forget puppy-proofing protocols if you do not have a dog.

Emergency Supplies and Disasters

In hot weather, a stalled car can quickly become an emergency for your Newf. The following information has been adapted from the NCA website, which provides detailed materials about managing emergencies and disasters. Here are the basic emergency items to keep packed in your Newf travel vehicle:

- An old cell phone and charger, which are good for 911 calls, should you forget your cell phone.
- A basic tool kit, including pliers, hammer, screwdrivers, common wrenches, and jumper cables—even if you don't know what to do, someone stopping to assist you may be able to help.
- Items to keep your dog secure and protected from heat:
  - Reflective solar blanket
  - Tarps
  - Battery-powered fan
  - Sunshades for vehicle windows
  - Water
- Items to assist emergency workers:
  - Easily visible envelope with emergency contact information and phone numbers of people to notify for help with you or your dogs
  - Crate to keep dog secured, allowing emergency workers to do their jobs
- Items to protect you and your Newf:
  - Brightly colored safety vest with reflective striping
  - Flashlights and/or headlamps
  - First aid kit
  - Wet wipes
  - Swiss Army pocketknife or multi-tool
  - Bolt cutters to cut open a damaged crate
  - Towels you can use for bleeding injury or as a sling to assist an injured dog
  - Rope, bungees
  - Duct tape

Disaster Planning

Be it wildfires, floods, hurricanes, or tornados, it is important to plan for your Newf's safety in the event of a disaster. You'll want to have a "go bag" packed with key items for your pet, including dog food, dog medicines, water, dog bowls, leashes, poop bags, dog vaccination records, and emergency numbers for the veterinarian and friends that can help care for your dogs. Post your dog instructions on the refrigerator, too, just in case you are not there for any reason during an emergency.

The NCA also recommends detailed disaster training for your dog. See checklist.

Disaster Preparedness Checklist for Pets

Ongoing Tasks:
Each dog has completed an basic manners/obedience class.
Each dog or cat will come when called.
On pet's birthday (or adoption anniversary date), schedule appointment with the veterinarian for a physical check-up and routine vaccinations.
Keep each pet's weight within the normal range.
All chronic medical conditions are closely monitored and treated.

Preparedness:
Prepare emergency notebook.
Accumulate emergency supplies, update every 6 months.
Learn about emergency care, take Red Cross Pet First Aid class.
Practice tasks listed in chart below

Task	Dates Practiced				Comments
Pet walking on leash/harness					
Pet coming when called					
Pet loading into carrier					
Pet accepting muzzle					
Handle and check pet's full body					
Giving pet a pill					
Giving pet liquid medication					
Lifting pet onto table					
Getting pet to load into car					
Evacuation drill					
Total time for evacuation					
Other:					
Other:					
Other:					

1. Emergency Contact who will care for pets: _____
Address: _____
Phone numbers: _____, _____
Interacted with pets on: (list dates) _____, _____, _____, _____

2. Back-Up Emergency Contact who will care for pets: _____
Address: _____
Phone numbers: _____, _____
Interacted with pets on: (list dates) _____, _____, _____, _____

 Courtesy of the Newfoundland Club of America, Inc. • Protecting the Newfoundland Dog since 1930. • www.ncanewfs.org

CHAPTER 15
The Older Newfoundland

> "
> *The old dog barks backwards without getting up.*
> *I can remember when he was a pup.*
>
> ROBERT FROST
> *The Span of Life*
> "

Robert Frost's poem indeed encapsulates the span of life with a dog: the brevity of a dog's life compared to humans, the rasping of an old dog's bark, the older dog who doesn't get up, and the intense memories of the joys of puppydom. It's bittersweet knowledge that you will probably outlive your cherished pet. According to John Homans, dogs have been mythologized as harbingers of death who know the way to the next world—the hounds of hell, the supernatural black dogs, and even a Connecticut black beast who makes no sound and leaves no paw prints all prophesy death. Some indigenous peoples believe a dog guards the bridge to the afterlife in the Milky Way, while Cherokee storytellers describe the Milky Way as cornmeal that fell out of a dog's mouth after it stole grain.

Life Expectancy

A Newfoundland has an average life expectancy of eight to 10 years, but many healthy Newfs live much longer. Some Newfoundlands have lived until 15 years of age, and dogs who reach 10 years proudly participate in a veteran's parade at the National. Count yourself lucky to live with an older, veteran dog. When your Newf reaches seven, she will be well into middle age and starting her anticipated three years as an "old dog."

Photo Courtesy of Katie Dolan

Signs of Physical Aging in Your Newf

Some of the things you might notice as your dog ages:

- Her habits and behaviors will change. Her digestive system may slow down, and she may have issues with bladder control. Talk to your veterinarian about medications that might help with incontinence.

- She may have difficulty getting up from the floor or favor one leg. She may develop arthritis or other health issues. She may benefit from the range of joint pain medications now available. Ask your veterinarian about treatment options.

- Look for changes in her eyes; cataracts are common as dogs age. You may notice a bluish haze on her pupils. Cataracts can develop in both young and old dogs and can result from diabetes. Surgical removal of cataracts is an option if your Newf is otherwise healthy. Should your dog's eyesight begin to fail, walk around your home, and remove potential hazards. A resource guide for owners is also available (See Resources chapter).

- Check her teeth and gums; older dogs and overweight dogs are more likely to have periodontal disease.

- Her hearing may decline. Hopefully, you will have taught her both verbal and visual obedience cues so you can communicate with her. At the same time, noise sensitivity (to fireworks and thunder) increases with age.

- Her stamina, strength, and flexibility will probably begin to decline, and you'll want to adjust her routines and activities. Newf groomer and breeder Becky Reynnells notes the older Newfoundland may have difficulty standing for a long grooming session and will be happier and better served by a slightly shorter coat.

- She will be susceptible to gaining weight. To keep your older dog trim, you may need to find a dog food with less protein but of higher quality.

After age 7, your senior Newf should have blood work and a veterinary check up every six months.

Emotional and Mental Changes

Older dogs show more pronounced stress reactions than younger dogs but have learned to control these emotions better, according to fascinating research using the Strange Situation Test. The test, originally developed to study attachment between children and their caregivers, was applied to adult and senior dogs. The study found older dogs were more passive and less interested in interacting with strangers during separation from their pet parents. Their saliva also had higher levels of stress cortisol. Older dogs were comforted by and more dependent upon their owners. According to the researchers, this may account for separation anxiety when it occurs in an older dog. So be sure to spend more time with your dog; remember to give her extra pats and belly scratches. Your older dog will appreciate the time with you even more than a younger dog.

Research also suggests dogs' personalities change as they age; they become both less active and less curious, according to a recent study of Border Collies. Dogs were tested with an exploration of the room, tempted by a sausage out of their reach, assessed for their reaction to a motorized toy, tested for ball fetching and basic obedience commands made by their owner, and underwent a lid-removal problem-solving test. The dogs were retested as they aged; both their problem-solving ability and curiosity about the novel object declined. The age of the dog was the strongest predictor of calmness, with older dogs generally being the calmest. On the other hand, old age and related infirmities can sometimes result in noise sensitivity, more barking, stranger-directed aggression, dog-directed aggression, fear of surfaces/heights, and insecurity.

Sleeping and Dreaming

According to dog expert Stanley Coren, giant-breed dogs like Newfoundlands have longer dreams but dream less frequently than smaller dogs. As I watch 10-year-old Blue stretch out on his favorite couch and fall asleep, I wonder whether he remembers the other puppies in his litter. Is he reliving the play matches with Willow when he lies on his back and allows her to jump on him? Is he dreaming about wading in the tidal pool near our house? Is he remembering a cross-country road trip when he and Bella stayed with us in an Airbnb with many cats? I watch him snore, and it sure looks like he's dreaming happy dreams as an old dog.

Nutrition for Seniors

A large study of pet owner attitudes and knowledge about canine nutritional issues for older dogs found that 42% of those surveyed fed a senior-based diet based on their perceptions that the senior dog food was lower in calories, protein, sodium, and carbohydrates (Hutchinson et al. 2011). However, the brands varied widely on these parameters. Additionally, there has been little research on the impacts of differing nutrients on older dogs. Most dogs require fewer calories as they age, but some research suggests older dogs experiencing changes in their taste or smell sensations or who have metabolic changes associated with disease may require more calories. So, the best advice is to talk to your veterinarian or breeder, watch your dog's body condition, and, if necessary, keep him trim by substituting green beans or carrots for a portion of his regular kibble or canned dog food.

Photo Courtesy of Katie Dolan

Regular Exercise

Changes in weight and activity levels are common in older Newfs, but regular physical activity is key to keeping your dog healthy and fit as she ages. That could be a walk outdoors, visiting a local dog park, socializing with other pets, or enjoying an indoor play session with you. Canine exercise should be fun. At least 20 to 30 minutes each day is recommended for physical and mental stimulation of your older dog.

Some older dogs may also benefit from flexibility exercises. You can consider Cavaletti rails, which are low poles set for a single step between the poles, or agility tunnels. In addition, figure-eight walking and (some) stair climbing can be added to your dog's routine to maintain strength, balance, and proprioception.

Helpful Devices

Items and treatments to help you care for your older dog include:

- Orthopedic beds
- Portable pet stairs and ramps
- Lifting harnesses
- Pet-friendly rugs
- Stair treads

Massage, Acupuncture, and Hydrotherapy

Talk to your veterinarian about these options for easing pain in your older Newf. Massage stimulates the release of endorphins and promotes blood flow, bringing oxygen to vital tissues and organs. A 2021 United Kingdom study found massage reduced the severity of muscle pain in dogs, while other research suggests massage reduces fluid retention in pets. You may want to use a professional veterinary clinic (see the ahvma.org website) or be trained in the Tellington TTouch (https://ttouch.com) method to give massages to your dog. Meanwhile, a 2017 study of acupuncture for dogs with neurological and musculoskeletal conditions found the treatments improved mobility in 80% of the 181 dogs studied.

In addition, hydrotherapy and underwater treadmills are effective in helping to build strength and muscle in dogs with musculoskeletal and neurological conditions. Some Newf owners take their dogs to hydrotherapy to keep them moving. A dog treadmill could be a great option for exercising your senior dog, especially if she doesn't have the energy or strength to play outdoors and go on long walks. Be sure to consider the treadmill's maximum speed, size, weight limit, and noise levels before purchasing a treadmill for your dog.

Saying Goodbye

In *Another Dog's Death*, John Updike writes, *"I took a shovel into the woods and dug her grave in preparation for the certain. She came along, which I had not expected. Still, the children gone, such expeditions were rare, and the dog spayed early; knew no nonhuman word for love. She made her stiff legs trot and let her bent tail wag. We found a spot we liked, where the pines met the field. The sun warmed her fur as she dozed, and I dug; I carved her a safe place while she protected me. I measured her length with the shovel's long handle; she perked in amusement and sniffed the heaped-up earth."* The human makes the preparations for an inevitable death; his old dog continues blissfully unaware yet still fulfilling her role as her owner's protector. Yes, we can anticipate and prepare, but when the time comes, so will grief. Acknowledge your loss, find support with friends, share stories, and remember when she was a pup.

Euthanasia and Hospice Care

"Euthanasia" is a Greek term meaning "good death." In this context, its objectives are met when death is induced which causes no pain or distress to an animal.

Your Newf will first be sedated to ensure the process is smooth, calm, and relaxed, with minimal stress. Euthanasia typically involves an intravenous (IV) pentobarbital injection, which quickly stops the heart. Pentobarbital used to be a common anesthetic agent; a hefty overdose is used for euthanasia. The most effective administration of the solution is through a vein, but a body cavity will also work, albeit not as rapidly. Your veterinarian will typically place an IV catheter in your Newf prior to administering the euthanasia solution. IV catheter placement allows easier venous access, making the injection process quick and painless, and minimizing complications.

Making Decisions When your Companion Animal is Sick, developed by the Argus Institute at Colorado State University, is a good resource to help you and your family as your Newf declines. It outlines strategies for caring for your dog, dealing with grief, preparing for euthanasia or hospice care, determining the need for a necropsy, helping children deal with the anticipated loss, reading children's books about the loss of a pet, and dealing with guilt.

How to Think about Euthanasia by Bernhard S. Hershhorn, DVM, offers relevant questions to clarify the difficult choices when your pet's health fails:

1. Is the condition prolonged, recurring, or getting worse?

2. Is the condition no longer responding to therapy?

3. Is your dog in pain or otherwise physically suffering?

4. Is it no longer possible to alleviate that pain or suffering?

5. If your dog should recover, is she likely to be chronically ill, an invalid, or unable to care for herself as a healthy dog?

6. If your dog recovers, is she likely to not enjoy life, or will she have severe personality changes?

If your answers to all six questions are "yes," the dog should probably be euthanized. If the answers to #3 and #4 are "no," perhaps the dog should be allowed to die naturally. However, you must then answer three more questions:

1. Can you provide the necessary care?

2. Will such care so interfere with your own life as to create serious problems with you and your family?

3. Will the cost involved become unbearably expensive?

Some owners choose to provide hospice care to their terminally ill pets, although this is another area where people may disagree. According to Louise Kehoe, veterinary hospice emerges from a succession of visits to the veterinarian's office, where the caregiver becomes familiar with therapies and procedures, including pain management. A vet technician may also make home visits for hospice care. Euthanasia may remain an option, but efforts are made to keep the pet pain-free so it can die a natural death at home, surrounded by familiar smells and people. In addition, many veterinarians will do a home visit to euthanize a dog. A growing number of veterinary practices have "hospice rooms" where you can spend time with your dog and let the staff know when you are ready for them to administer the IV and euthanasia drug. You are allowed to stay with your canine companion as long as you need.

Please remember that euthanasia procedures are also difficult for veterinary staff. Veterinarians frequently encounter situations where treatment options are available for a pet, but the owner does not have the financial resources to pay for care. In addition, veterinarians often graduate from school with extensive debt and have been grappling with staffing shortages and COVID-related challenges. As a result of the stresses, female veterinarians are 3.5 times more likely to commit suicide than the general population, and male veterinarians are twice as likely. Be gentle with the staff, just as they are being gentle with your loved pet.

Remains, Memorials, and Grief Support

Disposal of your pet's remains (cremation, burial, or donation to a veterinary school) is a decision you'll need to make. If your pet is cremated, you can choose to have the ashes returned for burial in your backyard or safekeeping in an urn. There are a variety of memorial stones that you can purchase for your garden. You may want to consider donating your Newf's body to a veterinary school for research and student training. Several schools and programs offer grief counseling and support groups: several are listed in the References chapter.

Rainbow Bridge

In the past, I've taken our dogs to our veterinarian to have them put to sleep. It was painful and heart-wrenching, but we knew when the time had arrived. The endings were peaceful, even in the antiseptic environment of the vet's examination room.

Bella's passing over the Rainbow Bridge at 12 years old was different. She had a massive stroke just as we were arriving back at our home in Little

*Photo Courtesy
of Jessica Hoffman*

Compton. Bella didn't eat or drink, lying collapsed in the back seat of the car. Her son Blue enthusiastically jumped out of the car and pranced around, enjoying the familiar smells of the fenced-in garden. It was a late Sunday afternoon. Peter and I managed to roll Bella out of the car, but she could not move. I called a veterinary service that does house calls for these situations but was told that, with COVID, they were understaffed and could not send someone until three days later. I stroked Bella's head and ears (remembering some Tellington TTouch motions), talking to her in a soft voice and reminding her she was a good dog. It started to rain lightly, so we rigged a large tarp over her body. Bella didn't move, just breathed in a labored way. I brought blankets and a pillow to sleep in the car next to her so she would not be alone.

When I awoke to the slanting rays of an early sunrise over the water, she was gone. Dazed, I walked Blue around the block, getting used to Bella being gone. I happened to see our retired neighbor peacefully enjoying an early morning cup of coffee before his golf game. Even though he is not really a dog person, I enlisted him to help us get Bella's body back into the car to take her to be cremated. The neighbor was a sport, with an unusual story to tell his golfing buddies. I was glad a part of Bella lived on in her sweet son Blue. For the next several weeks, Blue was devastated and left most of his food in the bowl, crooning and keening in the backyard as he missed his mother. It was real grief. Do not doubt that animals grieve.

One final bit of advice: Be sure to pay attention to the grief process in all family members, including other pets. A breeder friend recommended that I stay with Blue while he ate to make his meals feel a bit more like pack dining. So, that's what I did.

CHAPTER 16
Newfoundlands (and their people) in the World

The NCA, Regional Clubs, and International Clubs

I've mentioned the Newfoundland Club of America (NCA) and its 25 regional clubs previously, but I want to emphasize the value of these organizations to a new Newfy owner. The NCA recently published a strategic plan calling for expanded efforts to understand the health issues faced by Newfoundlands, attract younger members, support breeders, and educate Newf owners and the public about the breed.

The NCA creates policies, maintains a database, and distributes information about the breed through a magazine, email newsletters, and a website (ncadogs.org). It also maintains a Puppy Referral database that can be obtained by contacting a Newfoundland Ambassador. The NCA's charitable trust secures donations, manages and distributes funding in support of research grants to study health issues affecting Newfoundlands, provides monetary aid for Newfoundland rescue assistance, and awards educational scholarships to junior Newfoundland fanciers. The NCA and regional clubs also organize conformation shows, obedience, rally, agility trials, carting, parades, backpacking, and junior showmanship competitions. Most of the regional clubs also have active Newfoundland Rescue Committees and events. Many of the regional events are open to non-members as ways to educate non-Newf owners about the breed.

The Newfoundland Dog Club of Canada, https://www.newfoundland-dogclub.ca/events.html, has its own breeder list and referral system, local clubs, shows, and working dog events. The breed standard differs from the

Photo Courtesy of Katie Dolan

US standard in relation to permissible coat colors. Newfoundland owners in Europe can participate in the Kennel Club and the Newfoundland Dog Club, founded in 1886 in the United Kingdom, to establish standards for the breed.

Volunteer for Your Regional Club

A great way to meet other people passionate about Newfs is to join your regional club and volunteer to help at one of their events. The local clubs always need people to assist in organizing events, whether title trials, social gatherings, banquets, conformation, rescue work, therapy dog work, contributing to a prize basket at the National, or sending out the local newsletter. Newfy folks are almost as gentle as their dogs (although they do not drool), and you will learn a lot about the breed.

Become a Newfoundland Ambassador

There are currently over 100 ambassadors ready to provide education and introduce new people to the breed. As an ambassador, I've met some wonderful PPOs (potential puppy owners) and enjoyed talking about the virtues of Newfs. Families come from all over Rhode Island to meet my dogs in our native garden. The dogs love visitors and all the attention, the kids love petting our Newfs, and the adults have a chance to ask questions about adding a Newfoundland to their family.

As you settle into life with your Newf, you might be interested in helping other Newfoundland owners learn more about the breed. If so, join the Newf Ambassador program. Using the NCA website, people search for a Newf Ambassador near them to contact with questions they have about the breed. Minimum requirements to be a Newfoundland Ambassador include:

- Being an NCA member in good standing for three consecutive years prior to the date of application.
- Having owned two or more Newfoundlands over a period of five or more years.
- Owning (or having access to) at least one Newfoundland that can be introduced to the public. This Newfoundland must have an exemplary temperament and be clean and reasonably well-groomed.
- Preferably belong to a Regional Club.
- Being able to converse intelligently about several aspects of the Newfoundland breed and respond to common questions about Newfoundlands.

If you are interested in becoming an ambassador after you've been an NCA member for a few years, go to the website (ncanewfs.org) and complete an online application form.

National Specialty

The National Specialty brings together several hundred dogs and their owners for conformation and working title events. It is generally held in early May each year at various locations. To learn more about the NCA National Specialty, visit (https://www.ncanationalspecialty.org). `

I attended the 2022 National and learned many things, including:

- How to teach your pup to drink water from a spray bottle so he can stay hydrated without the mess of wet jowls before going into the show ring.

*Photo Courtesy
of Katie Dolan*

- How hard the handlers work. A seasoned professional handler told me she had worn an odometer at a show and logged 40,000 steps in one day!

- How one top breeder couple has won so many times that they have a complete dinner service of the National Specialty Lenox China.

- How carting, obedience, and drafting events happen at all times of the day.

- How to make a stacking box for teaching a pup the correct stance for the show ring.

- How all dog breeds must be identifiable by the head alone and by the silhouette alone. Each breed is distinct in these ways, as well as in its ability to do the job it was bred for and temperament/character. (I attended Pat Hastings' informative talk for breeders and learned that dogs bred for snow have longer legs so they can escape from snowdrifts; a German Shepherd is like a portable fence and can effortlessly trot for miles; an Australian Cattle dog can kneel to "bite the dirt" and knows to nip only the weight-bearing leg of a cow.)

- How Charlie Bear treats (only three calories per treat) are a good option as they don't crumble in your pocket.

- How the whole effort depends upon volunteers organizing everything from celebratory parties with costumes, prizes, vendors with Newf products, and registration gifts. Volunteering to hand out ring favors was perfect for seeing the dogs and handlers up close and taking pictures!

Photo Courtesy of Katie Dolan

"

As a Newfoundland lover, the National Specialty is an event not to be missed. I remember attending my first National. I went alone with my first Newf. He was just one year old. Arriving at the site, I saw a sea of Newfoundland dogs and instantly got chills seeing the beauty of all of them. I recognized Newf owners and handlers who I saw in magazines who lived all over the country and the world. There were so many Newfoundland items for sale in the vendor tents. I watched draft tests, obedience, and conformation, saw the rescue dog parade and the event that honored the oldest living Newfoundlands.

To this day, the event I still say is not to be missed is the Top 20 event. It's a fun showcase of the top Newfoundlands (show and obedience winners) in the country where they strut their stuff, and you can pet them and go over to each dog afterward. I had never seen such beautiful beings in my life and every year have made it a point to attend the Top 20 event and cheer for them, never thinking I'd ever have a dog as beautiful. I am so thrilled and honored to have had my dog Finnegan in the Top 20 for the last three years, and we will be exhibiting in this fun event at the National this year. I welcome all of you to come cheer for him and give him some hugs and love afterward!

The National Specialty has made such a positive impact on my family and me. We attend every year, in every destination it is held. What an amazing time to share our love of Newfoundlands with others who feel the same about our special breed. I never leave without making at least one new friend. Truly an amazing week!

MEGAN GOLDIN
Newfoundland breeder and fancier

"

*Photo Courtesy
of Katie Dolan*

Social Media and Popular Websites

In addition to the organizational websites described above and social media posts, there are many great sites for Newfoundland owners to share their pictures and stories. Some of the larger, most active sites on Facebook include:

- The Newfoundland Dog Owners and Lovers Group: a large group discussing various Newf topics
- The Ephemeral Newfoundland: memorabilia and artwork celebrating the Newfoundland in history
- Goofy Newfy: owners sharing pictures and advice about Newfoundlands
- Newfwise: general info and discussions
- Newf-L: issues and discussions
- The Best NewfGroup Ever: pictures and discussions
- Newfoundland Dogs Europe
- Newfoundlands UK

In addition, My Brown Newfsby Jen Costello is a fun, informative blog with lots of helpful tips. https://mybrownnewfies.com

Pets, Wildlife, and the Environment

Researching and writing the Bella books (a series of informative illustrated books featuring endangered species from cougars to shorebirds to coral reef inhabitants) narrated by my Newfoundlands, I discovered pet owners are indeed predisposed to live peaceably with wildlife. According to research, pet owners are more likely to feel egalitarian with wild animals. Childhood pet ownership is associated with an adult concern for wild animals, while farmers who have pets show more positive attitudes toward large carnivores. A Norwegian study finds pet owners exhibit more favorable attitudes toward 24 different wild species, although both pet owners and non-pet owners had equally strong negative views toward rats, snails, beetles, and mosquitoes!

So, how can pet owners help wildlife? In mountainous wild places, dog owners should be aware of and honor trail closures during elk migrations and breeding seasons. It is always good to keep your dogs leashed or in voice control to avoid prickly situations with porcupines and other wildlife.

Attention Dog Owners:
Dogs must be leashed and waste picked up and properly disposed of.
Attention Dogs:
Grrrr, bark, woof, ruff. Good Dog.
City of Minnetonka
Ordinance 1135.020

In the proud tradition of famous Newfoundland rescue dogs, we now need to find ways to rescue our remaining wild creatures. A first step is to take the BARK pledge, with four dog owner activities to help shorebirds and other wildlife:

- **B**= Bag waste
- **A**= Always leash in wildlife-sensitive areas
- **R**= Respect wildlife
- **K**= Know which beaches permit dogs

The Future of the Breed

Breeding a Newfoundland with another great Newfoundland to preserve the wonderful temperament and characteristics of the breed and improve the health status and longevity of future dogs is a very worthy endeavor. The NCA Health and Longevity Committee works to give reputable breeders the information they need to make good choices and maintain genetic diversity in the breed. It is also important to realize that many of the current top breeders are getting older; mentoring of younger people interested in preserving the breed is critical.

There have been recent discussions about whether selective breeding for a very defined stop and a shorter muzzle might become detrimental

Photo Courtesy of Katie Dolan

Photo Courtesy
of The Zimmerman Collection

for Newfoundlands in the long run. Carol Beuchat, a PhD from the Institute of Canine Biology, suggests Newfoundlands may become brachycephalic (with upper airway abnormalities causing partial obstruction to a dog's breathing) like French Bulldogs and some Spaniel breeds. A smaller muzzle may mean the dog has less ability to pant and cool itself. Also, the brain could get pushed too close to the spine, with resulting neurological disorders and breathing difficulties. Others in the Newf community vehemently disagree with this assessment.

Crossbreeding of Newfoundlands with other breeds will not necessarily produce the expected results in future litters. Decades ago, Jasper Rine, a genetics researcher at Berkeley with the Dog Genome Project, bred a Border Collie named Gregor with a Newfoundland named Pepper to assess which traits were inherited. On one extreme was the easygoing, affectionate, not easily startled, less active Newfoundland, contrasting with the Border Collie, who was intense, focused, easily startled, and likely to "show eye" or stare in a dominant way. Pups in the first-generation litter (F1) fell somewhere in the middle of the two breeds on measures of demand for affection, excitement barking, startle response, sociability with other dogs, and likelihood to stare. The F2 generation, however, exhibited nearly every combination of these characteristics. The study concluded that subsequent generations can be quite unpredictable in both temperament and physical characteristics.

I hope this book inspires you to find, cherish, and care for your own Newfoundland. You may also decide to work with your dog in various ways, to show her or even breed her. I've included a detailed description of our family's experiences with Bella's litter in the epilogue. Welcome to a special group of dog lovers.

The poem reprinted with permission below offers a lovely tribute to Newfoundlands of all ages:

Newfie Love

A ball of fur on four tiny legs
Was headed straight for my heart
She pawed and licked and bulldozed
Determined to win from the start

Impossibly cute and small
With bumbling silly ways
Before I knew it she was a giant
With a most inscrutable gaze

She stares at me when I'm eating
With a focus beyond compare
And my guilt increases with the dripping drool
– Now I ask you is this fair?

Her fur never stops spreading
It's settles all over the place
Stuck to the walls and ceiling
Even under the mask on my face

She follows me like a shadow
Sticking to me like glue
And when I'm not paying attention to her
She gets so very blue ...

She naps away most of the day
Snoring like a bear in the wild
But for some reason the sound is as comforting
As the sweet slumber of a child

She's a walking contradiction
Of awkwardness and grace
A magical blend of gentle and strong
Combine as one in her beautiful face

I can't imagine life without her
And I will never be the same
For I have been owned by a Newfoundland
A beast as wild as she is tame

Poem by Christine Mullis, Owner of www.newfielove.com

CHAPTER 17
Notes and Additional Resources

Chapter 1 The Versatile Newfoundland

Newfoundland Club of America website articles

Coren, S. (2006). *The intelligence of dogs.* Atria.

Bondeson, J. (2001). *Amazing dogs.* Cornell University Press.

Chapter 2 Breed Standard

NCA articles on website: www.ncanewfs.org

Chapter 3 Finding Your Newf

McMillan, F. (2017). Behavioral and psychological outcomes for dogs sold as puppies through pet stores and/or born in commercial breeding establishments: Current knowledge and putative causes. *Journal of Veterinary Behavior*, 19, 14-26.

Newfoundland Club of America website: www.ncanewfs.org. See "The Newfoundland Breeder Checklist" in Puppy Information Center

Orthopedic Foundation for Animals: www.ofa.org

That Newfoundland Place: https://thatnewfoundlandplace.org

National Newfoundland Rescue Network for Newfs and Newf mixes: https://nationalnewfoundlandrescue.com

Chapter 4 Preparing for Pup

Chwiecko, N. (2010). *There's a dog in the house: A practical guide to creating today's dog friendly home.* Design Dog Press.

Safe to Pets Rodent Control Options: https://www.raptor-sarethesolution.org

American Veterinary Medicine Association brochure entitled Pet hazards in your home and garden: www.avma.org

Chapter 5 Homecoming

Bergman, L., & Gaskins, L. (2008). Expanding families: Preparing for and introducing dogs and cats to infants, children, and new pets. *Vet Clinic Small Animals*, 38(5), 1043-1063.

Chapter 6 Training

McConnell, P., & Scidmore, P. (2010). *The Puppy Primer*. McConnell Publishing.

Dr. Ian Dunbar's Training Academy: https://www.dunbaracademy.com

Strickler, B. G. (2018). Helping pet owners change pet behaviors: An overview of the science. *Vet Clin Small Animals*, 48(3),419-431.

Jeannin, S., Gilbert, C., Amy, M., & Leboucher, G. (2017). Pet-directed speech draws adult dogs' attention more efficiently than Adult-directed speech. *Scientific reports*, 7(1), 1-9.

Wells, D. L., & Hepper, P. G. (1999). Male and female dogs respond differently to men and women." *Applied Animal Behaviour Science*, 61(4), 341-349.

de Castro, A. C. V., Fuchs, D., Morello, G. M., Pastur, S., de Sousa, L., & Olsson, I. A. S. (2020). Does training method matter? Evidence for the negative impact of aversive-based methods on companion dog welfare. *PloS one*, 15(12), e0225023.

Casey, R. A., Naj-Oleari, M., Campbell, S., Mendl, M., & Blackwell, E. J. (2021). Dogs are more pessimistic if their owners use two or more aversive training methods. *Scientific Reports*, 11(1), 1-8.

Horowitz, D., Ciribassi, J., & Dale, S.(2014). *Decoding your dog*. Houghton Mifflin Harcourt

Adriana Jakovcenic et al. (2010). Breed differences in dogs' (Canis familiaris) gaze to the human face. *Behavioral Processes*, 84.

Chapter 7 Exercise

Řezáč, P., Viziová, P., Dobešová, M., Havlíček, Z., & Pospíšilová, D. (2011). Factors affecting dog–dog interactions on walks with their owners. Applied Animal Behaviour Science, 134(3-4), 170-176.

Leaver, S. D. A., & Reimchen, T. E. (2008). Behavioural responses of Canis familiaris to different tail lengths of a remotely-controlled life-size dog replica. Behaviour, 145(3), 377-390.

Chapter 8 Socialization

Lord, K. (2013). A comparison of the sensory development of wolves (Canis lupus lupus) and dogs (Canis lupus familiaris). *Ethology*, 119(2), 110-120.

Cutler, J. H., Coe, J. B., & Niel, L. (2017). Puppy socialization practices of a sample of dog owners from across Canada and the United States. *Journal of the American Veterinary Medical Association*, 251(12), 1415-1423.

Pluijmakers, J. J., Appleby, D. L., & Bradshaw, J. W. S. (2010). Exposure to video images between 3 and 5 weeks of age decreases neophobia in domestic dogs. *Applied Animal Behaviour Science*, 126(1-2), 51-58.

Adler, J. (2019). *The Newfoundland puppy; early care, early training.* Self-published by J. Adler. Order at Sweetbay.com

Dietz, L., Arnold, A. M. K., Goerlich-Jansson, V. C., & Vinke, C. M. (2018). The importance of early life experiences for the development of behavioural disorders in domestic dogs. *Behaviour*, 155(2-3), 83-114.

Photo Courtesy of Katrina Wright

Wells, D. L., & Hepper, P. G. (1999). Male and female dogs respond differently to men and women. *Applied Animal Behaviour Science*, 61(4), 341-349.

Chapter 9 Nutrition

Freeman, L., & Chandler, M. L. (2013). Current knowledge about the risks and benefits of raw-meat based diets for dogs and cats. Journal of the American Veterinarian Association, 243(11).

Veterinary Nutritionist at Cummings School of Veterinary Medicine: www.petfoodology.org

How to assess body condition score

1.   https://wsava.org/wp-content/uploads/2020/01/Body-Condition-Score-Dog.pdf

2.   https://www.youtube.com/watch?v=tf_-rwxqHYU

Pet Nutrition Alliance. https://petnutritionalliance.org/

Pet Nutrition Alliance Dare to Ask

https://petnutritionalliance.org/site/pnatool/dare-to-ask-we-did/

World Small Animal Veterinary Association Guidelines for Selecting Pet Food: https://wsava.org/wp-content/uploads/2021/04/Selecting-a-pet-food-for-your-pet-updated-2021_WSAVA-Global-Nutrition-Toolkit.pdf

Board Certified Veterinary Nutritionists: American College of Veterinary Internal Medicine

www.acvn.org/directory

Wynn, S. (2013). *Feeding large breed puppies.* Innovative Veterinary Care. https://ivcjournal.com/feeding-large-breed-puppies/

Dodds, J. (2019, February 17). *Plastic, stainless steel, stoneware, silicone, or ceramic bowls.* doberman-chat.com

Case, L. P. (2021, November 22). *Human grade dog food: What you should know.* Whole Dog Journal. https://www.whole-dog-journal.com/food/human-grade-dog-food-what-you-should-know/

Chapter 10 Health

Orthopedic Foundation for Animals website: www.ofa.com. For health information on specific dogs

Newfdoghealth.org is a great website with presentations on health conditions in Newfoundlands. See Spay/Neuter link to Morris Animal Foundation talk with Dr. Missy Simpson, Study Epidemiologist for the Golden Retriever Lifetime Study, 2019.

Vaccines: Jean Dodds' site: https://hemopet.org/category/infectious-diseases-vaccines/

Natural health solutions for your Newf: The Whole Dog Journal: http://whole-dog-journal.com

Vetvine: vetvine.com offers a pet health library and resources for pet owners. See Dr. Rozanski's "Bloat: What Every Dog Owner Needs to Know lecture," 2020.

Orthopedics Foundation of America. Breed Statistics for Newfoundland: www.ofa.org

Reist-Marti, S. B. (2012). Genetic evidence of subaortic stenosis in the Newfoundland dog. Veterinary Record.

Lenner, L. A. (2022) The importance of eye checks. *Newf Tide.* Vol. 1

Hagman, R. (2022). Pyometra in small animals 2.0. *Veterinary Clinics of North America: Small Animal Practice*, 48(4). 639-661

Girault, C., Priymenko, N. Helsly, M., Duranton, C., & Gaunet, F. (2022). Dog behaviors in veterinary consultations: Part 2. *The Veterinary Journal*, 281.

Hart, B. L., Hart, L. A., Thigpen, A. P., & Willits, N. H. (2020). Assisting decision-making on age of neutering for 35 breeds of dogs: associated joint disorders, cancers, and urinary incontinence. *Frontiers in Veterinary Science*, 388.

Farhoody, P., Mallawaarachchi, I., Tarwater, P. M., Serpell, J. A., Duffy, D. L., & Zink, C. (2018). Aggression towards familiar people, strangers, and conspecifics in gonadectomized and intact dogs. *Frontiers in Veterinary Medicine*, 5(18).

White, A. M., Zambrana-Torrelio, C., Allen, T., Rostal, M. K., Wright, A. K., Ball, E. C., ... & Karesh, W. B. (2017). Hotspots of canine leptospirosis in the United States of America. *The Veterinary Journal*, 222, 29-35.

Kerns, N. (2022, April). *A new strain of tick-borne disease.* Whole Dog Journal.

Wells, K., & Smirniotis, F. (2021, August). *How to shop for the best pet insurance.* Wirecutter.

Wooten, S. (2021). Dog in heat: How to tell and what to do. BeChewy. https://be.chewy.com/preparing-for-a-dog-in-heat/

Ten Common Dog Accidents and Injuries. https://companionprotect.com

ASPCA Poison Control number: 888-426-4435

Chapter 11 Grooming

Adler, J. (2019). *The Newfoundland puppy, early care, early training*. Self-published by J. Adler. The book has great information including tips on grooming. Order at Sweetbay.com

The Newf Rescue Website (http://www.newfrescue.com/grooming-tips offers an illustrated guide by Iwonna Salak of Logrus Newfoundlands in Italy.

Chapter 12 Working and Showing Newfs

Adler, J. (2007). *The audible nose*. Self-published by J. Adler. Order at Sweetbay.com

Adler, J. (2009). *Water work, water play*. Self-published by J. Adler. Order at Sweetbay.com

World Canine Freestyle http://www.worldcaninefreestyle.org

North American Diving Dogs (NADD) https://northamerican-divingdogs.com

Hastings, P. & Rose, E. A. (2018). *Let's make you a winner: A judge's perspective on showing dogs*. Dogfolk Enterprises.

Chapter 13 Holidays

Salonen, M., Sulkama, S., Mikkola, S., Puurunen, J., Hakanen, E., Tiira, K., ... & Lohi, H. (2020). Prevalence, comorbidity, and breed differences in canine anxiety in 13,700 Finnish pet dogs. *Scientific reports*, 10(1), 1-11.

AVMA website: http://www.avma.org

Chapter 14 Traveling with Your Newf

The American Veterinary Medical Association website (www.avma.org) has a good FAQs about traveling with your dog as well as information on certificates of veterinary inspection and international/state laws on traveling with a dog.

Chapter 15 The Older Newfoundland

Homans, J. (2012). *What's a dog for?* Penguin.

Colino. S. (2021, November). The lowdown on alternative treatment for pets. *Better Homes and Gardens*.

College of Veterinary Medicine & Biomedical Sciences, Colorado State University. (2009). Making decisions when your companion animal is sick. https://www.cvmbs.colostate.edu/ce/making-decisions-when-your-companion-animal-is-sick-downloadable-pdf

Duranton, C., Bedossa, T., & Gaunet, F. (2016). When facing an unfamiliar person, pet dogs present social referencing based on their owners' direction of movement alone. *Animal Behavior*, 113, 147-156.

Dycus, D., Levine, D., Ratsch, B. E. & Marcellin-Little, D. J. Physical rehabilitation for management of canine hip dysplasia: 2021 update. *The Veterinary Clinics of North America*. Small Animal Practice, 52(3), 719–747..

Periodontal disease is more prevalent in small breeds and overweight dogs. (n.d). Banfield Pet Hospital Exchange. https://www.banfieldexchange.com/News/Periodontal-disease

Hutchinson, D., Freeman, L., Scheiner, K., & Terkla, D. (2011). Survey of opinions about nutritional requirements of senior dogs and analysis of nutrient profiles of commercially available diets for senior dogs. *Journal of Applied Research in Veterinary Medicine*, 9(1),68-79.

Abood, S., & Wara, A. (2020). Combining nutrition and physical rehabilitation to improve health outcomes for dogs and cats. *Advances in Small Animal Care*, 1, 239-264.

Association for Pet Loss and Bereavement: https://www.aplb.org

Allen, M. A. (2015). *Coping with sorrow on the loss of your pet.* Self-published by M. A. Allen

Chapter 16 Newfs in the World

NCA website: https://www.ncanewfs.org

Beuchat, C. (2017). *Please don't ruin the Newfoundland.* The Institute of Canine Biology. https://www.instituteofcaninebiology.org/blog/please-dont-ruin-the-newfoundland

Great Dog Books and Magazines

Whole Dog Journal: Informative articles about a range of canine issues. http://whole-dog-journal.com

Cox, L. (2022). *Tales of Al: The water rescue dog.* Knopf.

Coren. S. (2012). *Do dogs dream?* WR Norton.

Greer, K. (2006). *Pets in America.* Harcourt, Brace.

Horowitz, A. (2009). *Inside of a dog: What dogs see, smell, and know.* Scribner.

Kerasote, T. (2013). *Pukka's promise.* Houghton Mifflin Harcourt.

Kotler, S. (2010). *A small furry prayer: Dog rescue and the meaning of life.* Bloomsbury.

Lehrman, R. (1996). *In the company of Newfies: A shared life.* Henry Holt.

Olmert, M. (2009). *Made for each other: The biology of the human-animal bond.* De Capo.

Pryor, K. (2009). *Reaching the animal mind: Clicker training and what it teaches us about all animals.* Scribner.

EPILOGUE
Breeding My Bella

Research shows early experiences, even before birth, affect puppies: petting a pregnant female produces more docile puppies who have a greater tolerance to being handled when born. And, as we saw in the Socialization chapter, the first weeks of a puppy's life are critical for normal development. During the first two weeks, he is totally dependent on his mother for

nourishment, warmth, and elimination. Disease and mortality are higher for pups weaned at six weeks versus twelve weeks. A study of German shepherds found pups receiving a higher level of maternal care (nursing, licking, and physical contact) scored higher in engagement with humans and inanimate objects at eighteen months of age. Maternal care appears to influence the offspring's neuroendocrine and behavioral responses to stress, with effects lasting into adulthood.

Some readers may be considering breeding Newfoundlands. This epilogue describes our experiences when breeding Bella a decade ago and is for those who want to learn about breeding Newfs and how breeders socialize and care for young pups. The accompanying watercolors are by my good friend, Artist Judith Oskner.

I should emphasize that breeding a litter is expensive. Accounting for testing, veterinary appointments, stud fees, puppy clearances, puppy foods, equipment, books, vaccinations, and all the rest of the costs, it is generally a losing economic proposition. Good breeders are in it because they want to contribute to the overall health of the breed (and maybe because they really

love puppies!). Think carefully about the challenges and commitment before you consider breeding Newfoundlands. As you'll see, there are many highs and lows in raising a litter of puppies.

Breeding a purebred dog began with finding a breeder willing to sell me a puppy under a co-ownership agreement. Sue Auger of Denali Kennels was that person, and she graciously mentored me on the entire journey. Breeding also meant extensive testing when Bella was two years old. Her hips and elbows were checked, and she received an excellent hip rating – a score given to only eight percent of Newfoundlands at the time. Her heart was checked. Her thyroid was checked. Her eyes were checked. Both sire and dam were negative for cystinuria, so Bella was not carrying any genes for that urinary disease. I talked with Sue, Bella's breeder, about possible mates. She suggested McGee, a young male from Mooncusser Kennels since the kennel produces lovely big dogs. McGee had already received his AKC championship title.

Although she was unlikely to win any obedience or conformation titles, Bella would, I thought, be a good mother. She had grace, a calm disposition,

intelligence, excellent hips, and passed the other health clearances. Bella's whelp-
ing guides were her instincts and hormones; mine were friends, breeders, the
Newfoundland Club of America, and books. I studied canine fertility, puppy apti-
tude testing, and puppy development. Bella went into heat in early April. After a
few weeks of testing every other day, her progesterone levels suddenly skyrock-
eted. Suzanne, the stud dog's owner, suggested we come for a visit immediately.
We headed to the Cape, about two hours away. After navigating the Sagamore
Bridge, we drove down a dirt road, past scrub oaks and a blue pond, and arrived
at a modest house with a tall fence enclosing several woody acres. Large black
Newfoundlands barked gentle greetings through the fencing. Bella was cautious,
looking at the other dogs with interest and staying close by my side.

Suzanne opened the side door, saying, "Come on in. Is this Bella?" She ges-
tured at the room with a wooden whelping box, kennel, grooming table and
equipment, travel crates, tubs, 50-pound bags of dog food, and a laboratory
bench. "The Dog Room is the largest room in my home. It's where I spend most
of my time." She'd started Mooncusser in 1972, naming it in honor of local rum-
runners who coyly circumvented Prohibition's rules. The bootleggers, bringing

their precious cargo into New England's sandy beaches by boat at night, would cuss at the light of a full moon.

Suzanne is a well-respected breeder producing top-quality show dogs. Her dogs – huge, furry creatures -- are also known for their wonderful dispositions. "Bella looks nice and fit. Let's bring in McGee and see how they get along." McGee -- a massive male with a high forehead, beautiful eyes, and a heavy coat -- was ushered into the Dog Room. He clearly knew the stud dog routine and excitedly greeted Bella, licking her muzzle and rubbing up against her body. Susanne said, "Some bitches won't stand for a male – they get too aggressive and will even bite. But Bella seems fine. She's interested. Side-by-side Artificial Insemination is cleaner with less infection potential, and I can check the sperm before putting it inside Bella."

Quickly and with an experienced hand, Suzanne collected a semen sample, checked it under a microscope, added sperm enhancer, and injected it into Bella. She instructed me to sit down and put Bella's back haunches on my lap for ten minutes. Bella's front paws were on the floor as I fed her liver treats to keep her still. Suzanne commented Bella was beautiful but spoiled. "There's a lot to breeding, as you'll learn." Suzanne continued with sage advice on topics from natural whelping to calcium deficiencies to Lyme disease to safe exercise for a pregnant dog. As Suzanne talked, she opened the door to let McGee back outside. He reluctantly but obediently left. We soon heard high-pitched crooning as McGee led the other Newfs in a loud love serenade to Bella. It was an auspicious start to the breeding and whelping experience with my beautiful, spoiled dog.

On the advice of a breeder friend, I made an appointment with one of the handful of Canine Reproductive specialists. Dr. Truesdale, a tall, calm man, complimented Bella's looks and asked about the stud dog. He explained the reasons for planning a scheduled C-section -- less stress on the mother and fewer complications. For big dogs with large litters, the decision whether to free whelp or do a scheduled C-section is not made lightly. Free whelping encourages the mother's milk to come in, while C-sections make the delivery of many puppies more predictable. Sue Auger, Bella's breeder, told me a natural delivery is important and that Bella comes from a long line of healthy dams. I decided to base my decision on the numbers. If Bella has a litter of more than seven pups, we'd go for a C-section; if smaller, then we'd try a free whelping. The technician confirmed Bella was pregnant, with probably six pups. So, we'd plan a free whelping.

I called my breeder friend Linda to ask her to help, sent celebratory emails, and posted the happy news on Facebook and Bella's Blog. Then, I received a frightening phone call from Dr. Truesdale's office. The technician said, "Bella's

PEARLS OF WISDOM

Sue Auger, Bella's breeder, offered the following whelping pearls of wisdom:

- If a puppy is stuck, put Bella's legs up on something so gravity helps get the puppy out.
- Take Bella's temperature frequently. 102 degrees is normal; if temperature drops to 99 degrees, then delivery is imminent
- Give her lots of ice cream and treats
- Walk her up and down to encourage labor
- If she has the first puppy outside, be sure to have a flashlight to find puppy and a towel
- She'll take a long nap before she has her puppies
- It may take anywhere from 5 minutes to 2 hours between puppies
- Green discharge is a big problem and could be placenta separatus
- Don't cut the umbilical cord, let her chew it off
- Clear mucus away from the puppy's nose and mouth with a suction bulb
- Count the number of puppies and sacs; be sure they add up
- Help Bella open the amniotic sac and let her lick the puppy clean
- Let Bella eat the placentas
- Rub puppies with towel and both hands
- Put newborns in warmer (incubator) so they don't get stepped on by Bella; the temperature should be 90 degrees; only on low, never higher
- Don't leave puppies alone with Bella until they are at least 3 lbs. (3 weeks)

pregnancy is 'at risk' because she has anaplasmosis, a tick-borne disease. Bella needs to be treated with antibiotics." Walking on the beach with friends and their dogs, I tried not to obsess about Bella's diagnosis. Truesdale called and explained anaplasmosis generates an immune system response and is associated with pregnancy failures. "There is some chance the puppies might be reabsorbed." He prescribed three months of medicine for Bella and suggested another sonogram in a week.

I hung up and did a Google search for 'anaplasmosis and puppy reabsorption.' There were some hits but little research had been done. Puppies are typically reabsorbed between Days 28-40, only three to four weeks before they are due. I looked at haunting pictures of water puppies -- deformed stillbirths that can be born side by side with normal puppies. It was like reading an Obstetrics textbook while pregnant – not a good idea – so I turned off my computer.

Bella then got into calcium chews a guest had left by her bedside! I knew too much calcium could cause problems in pregnant dogs. Panicking, I calculated how many milligrams she may have eaten. I called "Ask a Vet" and was told possible liver problems could result. In the morning, I finally called Dr. Truesdale's office, and he reassured me that Bella would be fine. I don't think I worried as much during my two pregnancies and the whelping of our two sons!

As we awaited the long-anticipated birth, Bella dug a large nest under the hydrangea bush just outside the door, her black furry head wet with dew and her nose encased in brown dirt. The broad dark green leaves and the lighter green buds of the almost-flowering hydrangea camouflaged her distended belly full of puppies. Because she was high risk, Bella had a progesterone test every other day. Her levels dropped, and she slept a great deal – both signs of an imminent delivery. Dr. Truesdale suggested a progesterone booster shot so Bella would not go into labor too early. (Being born sooner than five days before the standard 63 days of gestation would be big trouble for the puppies.) After the shot, Bella's progesterone level soared. I breathed a sigh of relief.

My breeder friend, Linda, arrived. We double-checked the whelping room and supplies. Linda's advice included infection control procedures, the dangers of puppies eating garden pebbles, and creating separate areas for puppies to play, poop, and sleep. We spent Friday afternoon waiting and reviewing the whelping manuals. Bella's water broke just as we finished eating dinner. She was restless and wanted to dig anywhere there was dirt. First, she pushed through the front porch screen door and dug a Newfy-sized hole in the flower box. We brought her downstairs and showed her the waiting whelping box. Bella ignored the invitation and jumped up on the comfortable grey sofa where she normally snoozed.

Bella pushed and panted, running around to various parts of the room, but no puppy appeared. We worried. Linda, with concern in her voice, said, "If each puppy takes this long to appear, Bella will exhaust herself. She might not be able to get all the puppies out safely." We considered putting Bella in the car and heading to the emergency clinic. But then, a yellowish, opaque ball appeared. We massaged Bella's pubic area as the puppy slowly made its way out of her body. Soon a sac containing the first puppy was in a towel in Linda's hands. Immediately, we ripped the sac away from the puppy's face and let Bella lick the tiny creature. Then we suctioned the puppy's mouth and nose with a syringe. We cut the cord and tied it off with dental floss, then applied antiseptic to the wound. Bella happily ate the placenta.

The puppy, rubbed and dried off, got his blue Velcro collar, and was weighed (1 lb. 8 ounces). He was the size of a generous Idaho baked potato. He was

placed in the puppy incubator (a plastic bin with a heating pad on one side) as we awaited the next puppy's arrival ten minutes later. It was another male, the same size as Blue. Two minutes later, a smaller brown sac came out, a stillborn, fully formed but motionless. I suggested we put the body in the freezer for an autopsy, but my son wanted us to get rid of it. Linda stressed the dead puppy needed to be treated with dignity; my son volunteered to give it a burial at sea. He walked down to the beach in the fog, waded out into the cold water, said a short prayer, and released the lifeless body to the sea.

The stillborn birth shook us up -- suppose the other puppies still inside Bella were also dead? Twenty minutes later, a tiny puppy with a white chin and white paws appeared. She seemed weak as we rubbed and rubbed and rubbed, struggling to keep her alive. She weighed only 12 ounces. Her skinny legs and tiny black body were less than half the size of her siblings. Soon, another black male appeared, and then another small female, and then a big female. We had six puppies plus the stillborn delivered, so we assumed the whelping was complete. We helped Bella nurse her puppies, rubbing them and keeping them warm. Two hours later, Bella got restless again, and another male arrived, born out of the sac and needing lots of rubbing. Finally, another large female arrived at 2 am. She had a white blaze on her muzzle, a white chest, white paws, and a white tail tip. She was an "Irish spot" Newfoundland! An exhausted team of whelper-helpers, forever connected by eight tiny puppies, finally went to bed. Bella and her puppies slept too.

At first, the puppies were tiny, sightless deaf creatures that could not regulate their body temperatures. They could only smell and feel temperature changes. Puppies are not capable of finding their mother without thermal-tactile input.

The ear canal opens at about 20 days, but they do not reliably respond to sound until 25 days old. They twitch and sleep a great deal. They must be stimulated to urinate and poop; Bella licked their nether regions while I used a cotton ball dipped in warm water to get things going. One dog-rearing book notes puppies have close contact with one another in utero and are comforted by physical closeness. It urged us to cuddle the newborn puppies near our necks. The newborn puppy cannot see or hear but will feel the vibrations of our voice box. We did a great deal of cuddling those first few weeks. The puppies were so fragile, so vulnerable. I worried someone (or Bella) might accidentally step on a pup, so someone was always with her whenever she nursed.

I used moistened cotton balls to induce the puppies to tinkle and examined the tiny puppy poops. It was the best way to tell if they were getting enough to eat and drink. I weighed them every few days and adjusted the feeding schedule to make sure the runt of the litter was latched on more than the other pups. Those first few weeks, Bella and I developed a routine where we'd repeat feedings every three hours or so. She'd stand by my bedside and whine, clearly and concisely telling me it was time to feed again. I would mumble, "Okay, Bellarusse. Is it time to make the donuts?" Bella never got the joke, and we never had donuts in the middle of the night. By Week Two, the puppies learned to crawl towards Bella and latch on to her teats. By Week Three, their eyes opened. Puppies have blue eyes from lack of pigment -- like blue reflecting water – and only develop colors in their irises later.

Bella allowed her pups to nurse longer if she was entertained in the whelping box. As I fed her ice cubes, one by one, I thought about the Wildlife Conservation Society's animal enrichment program and remembered the distractions offered to a zoo gorilla undergoing heart surgery. The veterinarians did not want him to pick at the sutures on his chest when he woke up. They put gum in his fur, painted his toenails pink, and put other sutures in his pads. The groggy gorilla, happily entertained and distracted in the recovery room, recovered without playing with his chest sutures.

Over time, though, the little puppies grew sharp teeth. Bella didn't want to get up in the middle of the night only to be teat-terrorized by tiny teeth. So, we bottle-fed the puppies, or at least the ones who would take a bottle. Some absolutely refused the bottle; others would suck down three ounces in a minute. Soon,

Bella weaned the puppies down to an occasional walk-by suckle, then impatiently jumped out of their play area. By Week Four, the puppies happily lapped formula mixed with ground kibble, and by the fifth week, they were completely weaned. I made a clicking sound when delivering the meals – familiarizing the puppies with the sound of a clicker and associating it with wonderful things.

One day, during a Skype video call from the puppy room with my friend, I got up to show one of the puppies and tripped over the side of the whelping box. I tightly held one of the puppies as I tumbled to the floor, like a wide receiver in the Super Bowl making a dramatic catch. I did not let go, and Briggs was fine, but I had a giant bruise on my leg. It was a reminder of how easy it would be for a little puppy to get hurt.

Each night, we had cocktails with a different puppy on the front deck. Everyone made a fuss as the chosen pup explored a small vegetable garden box and sampled happy hour cheeses. Research by Lord and others suggests many new experiences should be provided to younger puppies since a fear period begins at approximately eight weeks.

Although puppies should be exposed to new things during this critical social-ization period, there is a tradeoff because you want to minimize exposure to germs. I'll admit to being obsessive: I knew an entire litter could succumb to a single wayward parvovirus exposure. Awake in the middle of the night between feedings, I worried about why the puppies cried, when it was safe to switch from distilled to regular tap wa ͟r. and about infections. With young puppies, cleanliness is key. I asked the agreeable gardeners to take off their shoes while working where the puppies played; I asked guests to either remove their shoes or step into a Clorox-laced basin before coming into the house. I asked every visitor to use antibacterial wipes before picking up a puppy. I don't recall having the same requirements when people came for our kids' christenings!

The puppies loved snoozing underneath things – perhaps it reminded them of their time in Bella's packed abdomen full of puppies. They loved being outside, even in rainy weather. They often slept right in the water bowl, with a wet ear dangling in the bowl. A wet paw or wet chest felt delightful during a summer snooze. In fact, the males seemed to sleep more than the females. Sue, the breeder, explained, "They are doing just what they are supposed to do. The males are growing fast and resting; the girls are more active and do all the work. It's like the human gender gap." At about four weeks, puppies are capable of barking, but they rarely did. Barking is displayed by dogs who are conflicted or not sure

what to do. These puppies had few conflicts in their little lives, except for play fights with littermates.

Blaze had a thick white strip down her nuzzle, several white paws, a white tail, and a broad white chest. She was the largest female, gentle, and cuddly. Sunshine spent her days wrestling with her four brothers – she was spunky, loved to chew my hair, and was often in the middle of the puppy-piles. Sunshine was an early adopter of the bottle and sucked down three ounces in minutes. The smaller females -- Orangina and Weetamoo -- were inseparable. They fought and tussled. One morning, they escaped the puppy play area to investigate the adjacent bathroom, unraveling toilet paper and chewing on a toilet brush. They were also the first to wake up if a human visited; the first to run over and play. Blue, the puppy we decided to keep, was right behind them, wagging his tail and waiting to be petted.

The fourth weekly weigh-in had the puppies at 8-10 pounds, with Blue still the heavyweight. I dewormed them one night. It was best to weigh them when they were pooped out (so to speak) after a big meal – they fell asleep on the scale and didn't wiggle around as much. Our son's high school friends visited over the weekend: twenty teenage boys to socialize the puppies, play on the beach, and chase tennis balls.

Young eaters should have their meals provided in a wide variety of containers so that they are not afraid of eating in multiple settings. I suspected this will not be a concern with my Newfoundland chowhounds, but it was a good use of mismatched and chipped dishes. The pups were served on china plates as well as steel bowls. They preferred the china! Thinking of the "Puppy Rule of Twelve," we provided lots of new experiences as the puppies grew. One day, we focused on different walking surfaces -- a rough flagstone path in the garden, grass, pebbles, and the hard tennis court.

Whenever we went outside, the puppies followed. It was like having an entourage! The Pupperatizi are following! We gave the puppies their first swimming lesson in a wading pool. My husband Peter gently placed one of the females in the warm, shallow water. The pup stood still, not sure what to do. We quickly washed and dried her, then returned her to the safety of dry ground. During their next swim, the puppies splashed and walked around the plastic pool, becoming swimmers slowly by getting used to the water. Meanwhile, Bella looked wistfully towards the ocean and her favorite tidal pool swimming spot. Unfortunately, she needed to wait until she healed from the birth of eight puppies.

The puppies chewed each other's ears, tails, paws, and neck napes. At first, heartfelt yelps and squeals punctuated the calm of summer afternoons in the sunlight puppy pen and outdoor play area. By testing their sharp teeth, the litter-mates quickly learned the outer limits for chomping fur and skin. Canine signals – a soft chew, a submissive gesture, a play bow, a raised tail, or an averted eye – created an established set of rules that would prepare the pups for their future canine encounters. Puppies learn such critical social skills only during a narrow window between seven and nine weeks of age; afterward it is much more difficult to absorb these playtime rules.

To create a Potential Puppy Owner (PPO) survey, I looked at what other Newfoundland breeders asked about their puppies. Bella and I wanted our pup-pies to be able to swim regularly. We wanted our puppies to play in a fenced yard, not within an often-ineffective electric fence. We wanted owners who would generally be home with their dog. We wanted the puppies to sleep near their humans. The potential puppy owners were of various breeds themselves. I gave the new owners a detailed Puppy Handbook with information on health clear-ances, vaccinations, puppy care, expectations about fencing, and a contract.

One man wanted to give his wife a Newf for her birthday and to see the pup-pies when they were only two weeks old. It was no surprise that they'd already

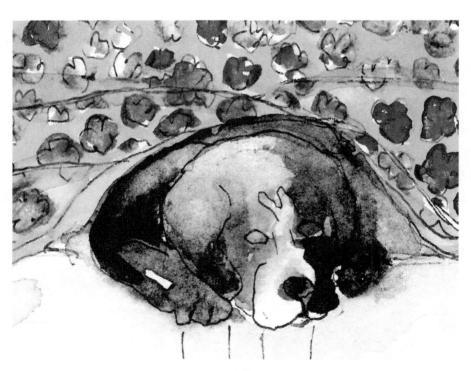

gotten a puppy by the time Bella's litter was old enough for visitors. Another family arrived with pictures of their previous brown Newf. They had auburn brown hair and asked many questions about Bella's coat. They were looking for a replacement for their previous dog -- I bet they ended up with a brown pup. Another family sent in a home video starring their precocious 10-year-old describing the family's love of its hamster. They even brought delicious Newfoundland-shaped cookies when they came to look at the puppies!

After the last puppy left with its new family, Bella, Blue, and I sat in the garden on an early September morning, surrounded by faded Beach Rose and Queen Anne's Lace. Even the hydrangeas had faded to a mottled pinkish-grey. Monarchs convened on a purple butterfly bush – their brown wings worn and torn. The garden and its insect inhabitants were as tired and frayed as Bella in her thin black coat. Her fur needed replenishment after a summer season of carrying, feeding, and watching puppies. In contrast, Blue was furry, as soft as the lavender blooms of Joe-Pye weed. Beyond the monarchs and Joe-Pye weed, Bella and Blue barked at each other. Blue challenged his mother, ran up, tackled and tussled with her, then flattened himself on the ground when she bossed him around. She was rough; a form of tough love which was uncomfortable. I talked to Sue, the sage breeder, about these behaviors; she claimed Bella already recognized Blue would be a dominant dog and was merely teaching humility to her pup.

I resolved to watch, intervening only when it got too rough. Simply sitting felt wonderful after a long summer of puppy-related activity. Author Alice Walker writes, "Change is a relay race, and we're very conscious of that. Our job really is to do our part of the race, and then we pass it on, and then someone picks it up, and it keeps going." We'd completed our leg of the relay race to raise these dogs. The dogs ambled over to drink water on the patio. Blue had already learned some tricks from his mom – how to barge through a screen door, how to drink coffee, and how to win his furry way into our hearts.

In a quiet house, the humans, Bella, and Blue developed new routines. At 9 p.m. each night, Bella sat down in front of me, whining softly and looking expectantly. At first, I thought she needed to go outside, but she did not react when I grabbed her leash. Then, it dawned on me. She was ready for bed and wanted me to join her. I said goodnight to Peter, put on my pajamas, brushed my teeth, lay down, and picked up a book. Bella jumped up on the bed, circled once, plopped down, and sighed contentedly.

Printed in Great Britain
by Amazon

21097353R00120